BOUNDLESS FAITH

Early American Women's Captivity Narratives

EDITED AND MILDLY MODERNIZED BY

HENRY L. CARRIGAN, JR.

PARACLETE PRESS

BREWSTER, MASSACHUSETTS

Library of Congress Cataloging-in Publication Data
Boundless faith : early American women's captivity narratives / edited and modernized by Henry L. Carrigan, Jr.
        p. cm. — (Christian classics)
Includes bibliographical references.
    ISBN 1-55725-339-0 (trade paper, perfect bound)
1. Indian captivities—United States—History. 2. Christian women—United States—Biography. 3. Rowlandson, Mary White, ca. 1635–1711. 4. Duston, Hannah Emerson, b. 1657. 5. Hanson, Elizabeth, 1684–1737. 6. Wakefield, Sarah F. I. Carrigan, Henry L., 1954– II. Title. III. Series: Christian classics (Brewster, Mass.)
    E85.B68 2003
    277.3'07'0922—dc21

                                                              2003012591

10 9 8 7 6 5 4 3 2 1

© 2003 by Paraclete Press, Inc.
ISBN: 1-55725-339-0

Published by Paraclete Press
Brewster, Massachusetts
www.paracletepress.com
Printed in the United States of America.

Contents

INTRODUCTION

In 2001, the world was startled when the Taliban government in Afghanistan kidnapped two American foreign aid workers. Held for several months, the women had been taken hostage because of their national and political identities. More important, the Taliban government objected to their religious views and was concerned that these women were promoting Christianity in a strict Islamic culture that forbade proselytizing. In their book, *Prisoners of Hope*, Dana Curry and Heather Mercer describe the three months of their captivity at the hands of the Taliban. Throughout their ordeal the women never lost hope or faith that God's providence would sustain them.

From the seventeenth through the nineteenth centuries, many Christian women had similar experiences. Living on the frontiers of a new world, these women found themselves confronted with a Native American culture about which they knew little, apart from stereotypical reports of native savagery. When violence broke out between the colonists and Native Americans in New England, the latter often captured the colonists, taking them back to tribal villages to replace warriors and others who had fallen either to disease or to war.

Some of these captives were women whose husbands were either ministers or governors in the colonies. Several of them wrote compelling narratives about their experiences, describing not only their captivity but also the ways that their faith in God was tested by this time. The most famous is Mary Rowlandson's *The Sovereignty and Goodness of God* (1682). In February 1676, Rowlandson and her three children were taken captive by a coalition of Native American tribes in Massachusetts. In the first few weeks of her captivity, her youngest daughter, Sarah, died from wounds she suffered during the abduction. Rowlandson was immediately separated from her other two children. In spite of these losses, she sustained herself by faith and will. Her account stands in the religious context whereby a person is removed, tested, and returned, then reflects on the ordeal, marking it as an act of providence. In turn, the captive's story becomes a source of inspiration, especially for those whose fears of the wilderness often overwhelm their faith in providence.

Although Rowlandson's account is the best known, other women had similar experiences and wrote about them. In 1702, Cotton Mather told the story of Hannah Dustan, whose captivity led her to seek the vengeance of God on her captors. The Quaker Elizabeth Hanson's *God's Mercy Surmounting Man's Cruelty* (1728) demonstrates the differences between God's love and justice and humanity's quest for revenge. By the nineteenth century, captivity narratives had taken a different turn, and Sarah Wakefield's description of her six weeks among the Sioux (1864) is notable for its condemnation of the hypocrisy and cruelty that she witnessed among certain white American Christians.

Each of the captivity narratives featured in this book offers inspiring accounts of God's providence at work in the world.

A Word About the Texts

I have remained true to the spirit of these texts, even where I have modernized them. Mostly, my modernizations have come in two areas: I have replaced archaic words and forms of address with more modern ones. Thus, "thou" and its related pronoun forms become "you" and its related forms. And I have altered the syntax and sentence structure of these texts to make them livelier and more understandable by a modern audience. Often this simply means casting sentences in the active rather than the passive voice. To avoid anachronism, however, I have not used the phrase Native American to refer to Indians. The authors of the captivity narratives knew their captives only as Indians, and sometimes called them savages or pagans. I have followed the authors' usage to retain the force of their own feeling about their captors.

When quotations from the Bible appear, they come from the New Revised Standard Version, unless otherwise indicated.

I have used the following editions in this book:

Mary Rowlandson. *A True History of the Captivity and Restoration of Mrs. Mary Rowlandson.* Fourth edition. London: Joseph Poole, 1682.

For Hannah Dustan: Cotton Mather. "A Notable Exploit" from *Magnalia Christi Americana; or Ecclesiastical History of New-England.* London: Thomas Parkhurst, 1702.

Elizabeth Hanson. *God's Mercy Surmounting Man's Cruelty.* Philadelphia: Samuel Keimer, 1728.

Sarah F. Wakefield. *Six Weeks in the Sioux Teepees: A Narrative of Indian Captivity.* Second edition. Shakopee, Minnesota: Argus, 1864.

These startling and powerful narratives help us to reflect on God's continuing role as caretaker and provider in our world.

Henry L. Carrigan, Jr.

A True History
of the Captivity and
Restoration of

Mrs. Mary Rowlandson

The Preface to the Reader

On the afternoon of Tuesday, February 1, 1675, the armies of the United Colonies defeated the forces of the Narrhagansets. The colonial soldiers pursued the Narrhagansets all the next day, destroying some of those that they caught. By Thursday, February 3, the English were tired, and their supplies were greatly diminished. About noon on that day, they convened a Council of War to decide what their next step should be. Although some disagreed with the Council's decision, it declared that they should no longer pursue the Narrhagansets. Each contingent thus returned to its own part of the country, but eventually this decision turned out to have dismal consequences because of the vengeance taken by these Indians.

The Narrhagansets had now been driven out of their country. They had left all their provisions in their homes, and they did not dare return to get them. Since they soon found themselves hungry and without food, they decided to provide for themselves by raiding the English supplies. Seeing that they were no longer pursued, with mighty force and fury they attacked the town of Lancaster on February 10. This small town was not near the others and was not surrounded by fortress walls, as others were. The Army was not able to get to the town in time to offer any effective resistance. Although the townspeople fought bravely, most of the town's buildings were burned to the ground. Many men, women, and children were killed, and others were captured.

The most remarkable part of this tragedy happened to the Reverend Joseph Rowlandson. When he returned from the Council of Massachusetts, where he had gone to seek assistance for the town, he found both the town and his own house on fire. His precious wife, Mary, and his dear children had been wounded and captured by the Narrhagansets. Thus both good and bad things happen to everyone, even God's chosen.

It is no new thing for God's precious ones to drink from the cup of calamity as deeply as others. But I do not want to spend much time on these things. I simply want to narrate the wonderfully wise, holy, powerful, and gracious providence of God. God cast me into a waterless pit, but he preserved and supported me, carrying me through many extreme hazards and unspeakable difficulties, and delivering me and my surviving children out of all these troubles. It was strange that the Lord put his precious follower through such torture and agony. It was just as strange that he would give me strength and keep my spirit strong as he did through all my trials, delivering and restoring me after I had endured them. But our God tells us: When you pass through the waters, I will be with you; and through the rivers, they shall not overwhelm you; when you walk through fire you shall not be burned, and the flame shall not consume you *(Is. 43:2). And as he tells us in Job:* For he wounds, but he binds up; he strikes, but his hands heal. He will deliver you from six troubles; in seven no harm shall touch you. In famine he will redeem you from death, and in war from the power of the sword *(Job 5:18–20). I think my story resembles those of Joseph, David, and Daniel, and the three children, too. These stories provide us with portraits of curious pieces of divine work and excellent examples of divine providence. Just as these stories do, my story teaches a lesson that should not be forgotten but considered by everyone who wants to ponder the operations of God's hands.*

I wrote this story as a reminder of the ways that God has dealt with me, so that I will never forget these events as long as I live. I had not intended to publish my narrative, but when some of my friends read it they were deeply touched by the many passages describing the workings of God's providence. They encouraged me to publish my story, because in their opinion the events I describe should not be hidden from our generation or from future generations. Because of my gratitude to God, I decided to publish it in order to praise God's glory and to benefit others as well as myself.

Those who have tasted deeply the goodness of the Lord will benefit from my story. I ask, as David did, What shall I return to the LORD for all his bounty to me? *(Ps. 116:12). David realizes that his own praises to God are inadequate, so he calls for help:* O magnify the LORD with me, and let us exalt his name together *(Ps. 34:3). In my story I focus on particular events in my captivity that caused me to pray to God for help and events that caused me to praise and magnify God's mercy. Like David, I have declared what God has done for my soul:* Come and hear, all you who fear God, and I will tell what he has done for me. *And in verses 9–10 David declares:* He has kept us among the living, and has not let our feet slip; for you, O God, have tested us; you have tried us as silver is tried *(Ps. 66:16, 9–10). The mercies we experience in our life affect our hearts. From these experiences we learn how to praise God and talk to others about his wonderful works. When deep troubles come into our souls we must talk about the ways God has delivered us. No one can imagine what it is like to be captured and enslaved to such atheistic, proud, wild, cruel, and diabolical creatures as these Narrhagansets. No one can imagine the difficulties, hardships, hazards, sorrows, anxieties, and perplexities that accompany such captivity. No one can then imagine how much I have to repay to God. With this story I confess publicly how much I owe to God's mercy; come and hear my story.*

I am confident that no one acquainted with God's providence will regret reading these pages. That person will find them worth reading over and over again.

In these pages you will see an example of God's sovereignty. You will see an example of the faith and patience of the saints, who experience the most heart-sinking trials. You will here see how God's promises are full of consolation when the world itself is empty, offering nothing but sorrow. You will see that God is the supreme Lord of the world, ruling the most unruly, weakening the cruelest and most savage. He grants his people mercy in sight of the most unmerciful, curbs the lusts of the lascivious, holds the hands of the violent, and delivers the weak from the mighty. Once again you will see the power that belongs to God. Our God is the God of salvation. From these pages you will see the ways that the Lord has taught me through all my afflictions. I can now say that it has been better for me to experience such trials in captivity than for me not to have had these trials. O how God shines in things like these.

If my story does not bless you, then it is your fault. Read my story; ponder it and save up some lessons from it for the time when you experience such adversity, so that through patience and the consolation of Scripture you may have hope.

The Narrative of the Captivity and Restoration of Mrs. Mary Rowlandson

On February 10, 1675, the Indians attacked Lancaster in great numbers. They first came about sunrise. We looked out when we heard the noise of some guns. Several houses were on fire, with the smoke curling toward heaven. In one house there were five people. The Indians had already killed the mother, the father, and an infant, and had carried away the other two children. We saw two other people attacked by the Indians; one was killed, and the other escaped. One person was running away, and he was shot and wounded. When he begged for his life, they did not listen to him but killed him. Another person went out into his yard when he saw Indians around his barn. He was quickly shot. The Indians got up on the barn's roof and had the advantage of shooting down upon all those below them. In this way these murderous wretches continued on their rampage, burning and destroying everything before them.

They soon came to our house, and it was the saddest day of my life. The house stood on a hill. Some of the Indians went behind the hill, others went into the barn, and others hid behind anything that would provide shelter for them. From all these places they shot against our house so that the bullets flew like hail. In a short time they wounded three men who were with us in the house. After about two hours, they set fire to the house. One of us went out and put out the fire, but the Indians set it again. Now came a dreadful time. Some in our house were fighting for their lives, others wallowing in their own blood. The house was on fire over our heads, and the Indians were ready to kill us if we went out of the house. Mothers and children were crying out to one another, saying, *Lord, what shall we do?* I then took one of my children, and my sister took one of hers, and we tried to leave the house. As soon as we got to the door, the Indians shot at us so heavily that the bullets rattled against the house as if handfuls of stones were being thrown against it. Even our dogs, which under other circumstances would have flown at the Indians and torn them apart, remained silent. Thus the Lord would make us acknowledge his hand and know that we always depend on him for his help.

Because the fire increased we had little choice but to leave the house and face our attackers. As soon as we were out of the house, my brother-in-law, who was already wounded, fell down dead. The Indians then came and stripped off his clothes. The bullets were flying thick as hail, and one went through my side and through the stomach and hands of the dear child I was carrying in my arms. One of my sister's children had his leg broken. Thus these merciless attackers butchered us, with blood running down to our heels. My elder sister was still in the house. When she saw these sorrowful sights and found out that her son William had been killed and that I was wounded, she said, *Lord, let me die with them.* No sooner had she said this than she was struck by a bullet and fell dead over the threshold. I hope she is reaping the fruit of her good labors, being faithful to the service of God in her place.

The Indians had laid hold of us, pulling me one way and the children another way. They said, *Come, go along with us.* I asked if they were going to kill me. They told me that if I were willing to go with them they would not hurt me.

What a sorrowful sight at our house! *Come, behold the works of the LORD; see what desolations he has brought on the earth* (Ps. 46:8). Out of the thirty-seven people who were in this house, none escaped either death or captivity, except one. Twelve were killed—some shot, some stabbed with spears, and some knocked down with hatchets. When we dwell in prosperity how little we think of such sights. There was one who was chopped into the head with a hatchet and was stripped naked, but yet was crawling up and down. It is a solemn sight to see so many Christians lying in their blood, like sheep that have been attacked by wolves. All of them were stripped naked by a company of fiends, roaring, ranting, and insulting as if they would have torn out our very hearts. But the Almighty Power of the Lord preserved a number of us from death. Twenty-four of us were taken alive and carried into captivity.

I had often said before that if Indians should come, I would rather be killed by them than taken alive. I changed my mind when I went through this trial. Their glittering weapons so daunted my spirit that I chose to go along with them rather than to end my life. So I can tell fully what happened to me during my grievous captivity, I shall speak of the several moves we made up and down the wilderness.

THE FIRST REMOVE

So we went away, our bodies and hearts wounded and bleeding, with those barbarians. We went about a mile that first night. On a hill overlooking the town where they intended to stay there was a vacant house. The English had deserted it because they were afraid of the Indians. I asked them if I could sleep in that house, and they mocked me, asking, *Do you still love Englishmen?* This was one of the most sorrowful nights I have ever seen. The roaring, singing, dancing, and yelling of these creatures in the night resembled hell. They wasted miserably so many of the provisions they had plundered from our town. The Indians were joyful enough, even though we were sad and beyond consolation. As if the previous day had not been sad enough and the present night not dismal enough, I could not stop thinking about my losses and my sad condition. Everything was gone. My husband was separated from me, and the Indians told me that they would kill him as he came toward home. My children, extended family, and friends were gone, and our house and home, with all its comforts, was gone. Everything but my life was gone, and I could not be sure that in the next few minutes even that might be taken from me as well.

All I had was my poor and wounded baby, and she was in such a poor condition that she seemed worse than death. My baby needed my compassion but I had none to give her; nor could I give her anything to revive her. These barbarous Narrhagansets are brutal—even though some of them profess to be Christians—when they have taken English settlers captive.

THE SECOND REMOVE

The next morning I had to turn my back on the town and travel with them into a vast and desolate wilderness. I could not know where we were headed. Neither my tongue nor my pen can express how sad my heart was and how bitter my spirit was when we departed. But God was with me in a wonderful manner, carrying me along and bearing up my spirit. One of the Indians carried my poor, wounded baby upon a horse, and my child kept moaning, *I shall die, I shall die.* I followed sorrowfully on foot. Soon I took her in my own arms, carrying her until I could do so no more. Then the Indians put me upon a horse with my wounded child in my lap. Since there was not a saddle on the horse, we fell off as we were going down a steep hill. These inhumane creatures laughed at us. I thought that right there we would die because we faced so many difficulties. But the Lord renewed my strength once again and carried me along, so that I might see more of his power. I would never have thought the Lord was this powerful if I had not experienced his power in this way.

After this it began to snow. When it was night, they stopped, and I had to sit down in the snow by a little fire. I continued to hold my child in my lap, and to comfort her, for she now had a violent fever because of her injury. My own wound was also growing so stiff that I could hardly sit down or stand up. I had to sit on the cold, snowy ground with my sick child in my lap on this cold winter's night, with no Christian friend near to comfort or help me. Because of God's wonderful power, my spirit did not sink under my helplessness. The Lord held me up with his gracious and merciful spirit, and we were both alive to see the light of the next morning.

THE THIRD REMOVE

In the morning they got up and were ready to move on. One of the Indians put my poor, sick child and me behind him on his horse. I had a very tedious day because of my own injury and my child's terrible sickness. Since we had not had any refreshing food or drink, except for a little cold water, from Wednesday night to Saturday night, we were very weak. On this afternoon we came to the Indian town called Wenimesset, where our captors intended to stop. Here a great number of Narrhagansets, who were now merciless enemies, surrounded me. I would have fainted if I had not maintained my strong belief in God.

The next day was the Sabbath. I then remembered how careless I had been in observing God's time. I had lost and misspent many Sabbaths and walked evilly in God's sight. These thoughts weighed so heavily on my spirit that I could easily see how righteous God was to cut off the thread of my life and cast me out of his presence forever. But the Lord continued to show his mercy on me, and he sustained me. Just as he wounded me with one hand, so he healed me with the other.

Later in the day I met another captive who had been with the Indians for a long time. He told me that he had been wounded in the leg during his fight with the Indians. His wound would not heal on its own, so he took oak leaves and wrapped them around his wound. With God's blessing, his wound began to heal. So I took oak leaves and dressed my wound, and with God's blessing my wound was also healed. But before the wound was cured I complained with the Psalmist, *My wounds grow foul and fester because of my foolishness; I am utterly bowed down and prostrate; all day long I go around mourning* (Ps. 38: 5–6). I spent most of my time sitting alone with my poor, wounded child in my lap. My child moaned day and night, and I had nothing to revive her physically or to cheer her spirits. The Indians were cruel to us, though, because they kept coming over to me saying that they would put my child out of misery by killing her with a blow to the head.

I had no comfort at all in this place, for the Indians were miserable comforters. I sat with my sick child in my lap for nine days, and my wounds opened again. When my child was close to death, the Indians sent me out to another dwelling. I think they did not want to be bothered by the spectacle of a loving mother comforting her dying child. I went to this new hut with a heavy heart, and I sat down holding this picture of death in my lap. About two hours into the night, my sweet child departed this world on February 18, 1675. She was six years and five months old. My child was sick, wounded, and miserable, without food or drink—except for a little cold water—for nine days. At any other time I could not stand to be in the same room as a dead person, but how different this time was. I had to lie down by my child's side all night long. Since that event, I have often praised God for giving me the presence of mind not to use violent means to take my own life. In the morning, when the Indians found out that my child had died, they sent me back to the hut of the Indian who owned me. I tried to carry my dead child in my arms, but they made me leave her in the hut.

After a while I took the first chance I could to go and look after my dead child. When I came to the hut, the body was not there. I asked the Indians what they had done with it, and they showed me where it was. They had dug a fresh grave and buried my child. So I left my child in the wilderness, and I committed her soul as well as myself—who also was wandering in this new wilderness—to God, who is above all.

Since God had taken away this dear child, I went to visit my daughter Mary, who was in this same Indian town. She lived in a hut not far away, but we did not have very many chances to see each other. She had been taken from our house during the attack, and later one Indian sold her to another for a gun. Mary was about ten years old, and when I appeared near her hut, she started crying. The Indians were upset about this, so they would not let me go near Mary and told me to go away from her. This broke my heart, for I had one child who was dead, another in the wilderness, and a third that they would not let me go to see. I felt much like Jacob who said, *I am the one you have bereaved of children: Joseph is no more, and Simeon is no more, and now you would take Benjamin* (Gen. 42:36). I could not sit still but kept pacing from one place to another.

As I was walking about, I was overwhelmed, thinking about my life. I prayed to the Lord and fervently asked him to consider my miserable state, and if it were his will to show me some sign of hope for my relief. The Lord answered me very quickly. While I was lamenting my situation, my son came up to me and asked me how I was doing. I had not seen him since our town had been destroyed, and I had had no idea where he was. He himself told me that he was with a smaller band of Indians, who lived about six miles away. Crying, he asked me whether his sister Sarah was dead. He told me that he had seen his sister Mary. He asked me not to be troubled about him. He was able to come to see me because his owner had gone out on with a war party to destroy a nearby colonial town. His owner's mistress brought him to see me. I took his presence to be the gracious answer to my fervent request.

The next day these Indians returned from their war party. The smaller party of Indians celebrated with roaring and whooping as they came through our town. The Indians in our town celebrated with them and congratulated the party on taking so many scalps of Englishmen. Even in the midst of this uproar, God showed me wonderful mercy, for he provided me with a Bible. One of the Indians in the war party had brought some plunder, and came to me and asked if I would like a Bible. I asked him whether or not the Indians would let me read it, and he said they would. So I took the Bible and I turned to Deuteronomy 28. Since my heart was already full of despair, my reading led me to believe that there was no mercy for me, and that the blessings were gone. But the Lord led me to keep reading until I reached the first seven verses of chapter 30. There I read that God promised his mercy to us again, if we would repent. Although we were scattered from one end of the earth to the other, the Lord promised to gather us together and turn all those curses upon our enemies. I cannot forget the deep comfort this scripture brought to me.

The Indians began to talk about leaving this place, with some of them going in one direction and some in another. Besides me, there were nine other captives: eight children and one woman. I had a chance to go and see them before we went our separate ways. The children all told me that they looked to God for their deliverance. The woman told me that she was planning to run away. I begged her not to do so, for any English town was at least thirty miles away, and she was expecting to deliver a child within a week's time. She also had another child, who was two years old. In addition, she would come to rivers that were impossible to cross safely. Since we had not received nourishing food and drink, she was also much too weak for such a journey. I had my Bible with me, and I asked her if she would read it with me. As if God were leading her hand, she opened it to Psalm 27:14: *Wait for the* LORD; *be strong, and let your heart take courage; wait for the* LORD!

The Fourth Remove

I now had to go away from the little company I had. I parted from my daughter Mary—whom I never saw again until after our captivity—and from four little cousins and neighbors, some of whom I never saw again. Only the Lord knows what happened to them. The pregnant woman was also with this company, but she came to a sad end. Her spirit was so low, and she was so miserable in her pregnancy, that she asked the Indians repeatedly if they would let her go home. They were so impatient and angry with her repeated requests that they stripped her and surrounded her. When they had sung and danced around her in a hellish manner for as long as they wanted to do, they knocked her and her two-year-old child out. They then threw them both into a fire and told the children who were with the party that if they complained about going home they would be killed in the same way. The children said the woman did not shed any tears but prayed the entire time she was being tortured and killed.

I traveled about half a day with my party of Indians. We settled in a desolate place in the wilderness where there were no huts and where no people had ever been. We came to this place in mid-afternoon, and we were cold, wet, hungry, and weary. We had no comforting place to settle except the cold ground, and we had no refreshment but our poor Indian cheer.

My heart was aching for my poor children, who were scattered in the forests among the wild beasts. I was light-headed and dizzy—either from hunger, hard lodging, or trouble, or all of these things. My knees were weak, and my body ached from sitting up both day and night. I can hardly begin to express how spiritually miserable I felt, but the Lord helped me to express it to him. I opened my Bible, and the Lord brought me this precious scripture:

Thus says the LORD: *Keep your voice from weeping, and your eyes from tears; for there is a reward for your work. They shall come back from the land of the enemy* (Jer. 31:16). This verse refreshed me like a sweet liqueur when I was ready to faint. Many times I have wept sweetly over this scripture. We stayed in this place about four days.

THE FIFTH REMOVE

I believe our party kept moving because the English army was near and was following us. We moved quickly, as if our lives depended on it, for a considerable distance. The Indians sent some of their best warriors back to hold off the English while the rest of the party escaped. The party marched furiously, carrying their young and their old. Some carried their elderly mothers. Four of them carried a large Indian upon a bier, but they had to take turns carrying him on their backs when we came into a thick section of the woods.

A little after noon on a Friday we came to a river. I tried to count the number of Indians in the party when we were all gathered at the river to cross it, but there were so many I could not do so. During our travels, they allowed me to carry a light load because of my wound. I carried only my knitting-work and two quarts of parched meal. Since I was feeling faint, I asked my mistress if I could have a spoonful of meal, but she would not give me a taste.

The Indians quickly began cutting down trees in order to make rafts for crossing the river. When I crossed over, I was able to sit upon some brush they had laid upon the raft. Because of this protection I did not get wet while crossing the river. Once again, God provided for me, for my body was weak and would have been further weakened by getting cold and wet. *When you pass through the waters, I will be with you; and through the rivers, they shall not overwhelm you* (Is. 43:2). Some of us crossed over the river that night, but it was not until the night after the Sabbath that we all were across safely. On Saturday the Indians boiled an old horse's leg, and we drank the broth.

During my first week among the Indians, I hardly ate a thing. The second week, I found that I was feeling very faint because I had eaten hardly anything. Even then, it was hard to swallow and keep down their awful food. By the third week, the food was pleasant and tasty, although I would think how my stomach would in earlier times have turned away from such food and that I would have starved and died before I would have eaten such things.

During these days I was knitting a pair of white cotton stockings for my mistress. I had not yet worked on the Sabbath. When the Sabbath day came, the Indians told me that I must work on that day. I asked them to let me rest on the Sabbath, and that I would do twice as much work the next day. They replied that if I did not work when they told me to, they would break all the bones in my face.

I cannot help noticing God's strange providence in taking care of those who do not know God. There were many hundreds of them—old and young, sick and lame. Many women had babies on their backs. They traveled with all their possessions, and yet they all were able to cross the river safely. On Monday they set their huts on fire and went away on this journey. On that very day the English saw the smoke from the huts and began pursuing us. Yet the river put a stop to the English pursuit. God did not give the English courage to cross over after us. We captives were not ready for so great a mercy as victory and deliverance. If we had been, God would have shown the English a way to cross the river, just as he had allowed the Indians to cross. *O that my people would listen to me, that Israel would walk in my ways! Then I would quickly subdue their enemies, and turn my hand against their foes* (Ps. 81:13–14).

THE SIXTH REMOVE

On Monday the Indians set their huts on fire and went away. The morning was cold, and a large brook with ice on it lay in front of us. Some waded through it, but others went along until they came to a beaver's dam and crossed the brook there. I was among the latter, and because of God's providence I did not get my feet wet. I went along that day, mourning and lamenting over my situation. I was leaving my own country farther behind and journeying into a vast and howling wilderness. I then understood why Lot's wife wanted to look back on the place she was leaving. We came later that day to a huge swamp, and we camped beside it overnight. When I looked around me I could see nothing but Indians, who were as thick in number as the trees. Here I was in the midst of this enormous company of Indians with no Christian soul near me. Yet the Lord preserved me safely. God has been so good to me and mine!

THE SEVENTH REMOVE

Following a restless and hungry night near the swamp, we had a difficult time the next day. The swamp lay far below us— like a deep dungeon—with a high and steep hill before us. Before I reached the top of the hill, I thought that my heart and legs would give out. Because I was faint and my body was sore, the day's difficult travel greatly challenged me. As we traveled along, I saw a place where English cattle had been. That somehow comforted me. Just after this we came upon an English path, where I thought I could have lain down and died. A little after noon we came to a deserted English village, where the Indians quickly spread themselves over the deserted fields to glean what wheat, corn, or peanuts they could find. I picked up two ears of Indian corn, but when I turned my back one of them was stolen. An Indian came along with a basket of horse liver. I asked him to give me a piece, and he asked with wonder if I could eat horse liver. I told him I would certainly try if he would give me a piece. When he did, I laid it on the coals to roast it, but before it was fully cooked, some Indians stole half of it from me. All I could do then was to take what was left and eat it half-raw with the blood trickling from my mouth. Even so, the meat tasted savory to me, for to the hungry soul every bitter thing is sweet. Seeing entire fields of corn and wheat forsaken and spoiled and the remainders given as food to our merciless enemies made me solemn. That night we had a mess of wheat for our supper.

THE EIGHTH REMOVE

The next morning we had to cross over the Connecticut River to meet with King Philip, the leader of the Wampanoags. Just as I was stepping into a canoe, the Indians suddenly cried out, and I had to step out of the canoe. I had to travel four or five more miles up the river to cross it. Some of the Indians ran one way and some another. I think that the Indians saw some English scouts and were thus disrupted.

As we traveled up the river, we stopped about noon to eat and to rest. As I sat among the Indians, I reflected upon my life. Unexpectedly, my son Joseph approached me, and we asked about each other's welfare. We both complained of our sorrowful situation and the great change in our lives. Once we had husband

and father, children and sisters, friends and relatives, house and home, and the many comforts of this life. But now we might say with Job, *Naked I came from my mother's womb, and naked I shall return there; the LORD gave, and the LORD has taken away; blessed be the name of the LORD* (Job 1:21). I asked him if he would like to read a verse of Scripture, and when I gave him my Bible he found this comforting verse: *I shall not die, but I shall live, and recount the deeds of the LORD. The LORD has punished me severely, but he did not give me over to death* (Ps. 118:17–18). "Look here, Mother," he said, "did you read these lines?" And I want to explain here why I mention these few verses of Scripture. Like the psalmist I want to praise the works of the Lord and his wonderful power in carrying us along and preserving us in the wilderness while in the enemy's hand, and returning us safely again. God expressed his goodness by bringing to my hand so many comforting scriptures during my distress.

We traveled until night, and the next morning we crossed over the river. While I was in the canoe, I could not help being amazed at the huge number of Indians on the other side of the river. When I came ashore they surrounded me, and I was alone in their midst. They asked one another questions, laughing and rejoicing over their victories. My heart then sank, and, for the first time that I can recall, I cried in front of them. Although I had already met with such sorrow and my heart was ready to break so many times, I could not shed one tear in their sight. But now, *By the rivers of Babylon—there we sat down and there we wept when we remembered Zion* (Ps. 137:1). One of the Indians asked me why I was crying. I didn't really know what to say, and I said that they would surely kill me. No, he said, none of us will hurt you. Then one of the Indians brought me two spoonfuls of meal to comfort me, and another gave me a half pint of peas, which was worth more than many bushels at any other time.

Then I went to see King Philip. He asked me to come in and sit down, and he asked me whether I would smoke a pipe with him. But smoking did not suit me. Although I had once used tobacco, I had given it up. I remember with shame how in the past, when I had smoked two or three pipes, I always wanted another one, for tobacco is so addicting. But God has now given me power over it.

The Indians were now gathering their forces to make a raid on Northampton. All night they were yelling and whooping to give notice of their plans. They boiled peanuts and corn as provisions, and they went away in the morning.

While I was living in Philip's village, he asked me to make a shirt for his son. I did, and he gave me a shilling, which I then offered to my owner. My owner told me to keep the money, and I bought a piece of horseflesh with it. Soon afterward I made a cap for Philip's son, and he invited me to dinner, where he served me a huge pancake that had been cooked in bear grease. I never tasted such pleasant food in all my life. A woman in the village asked me to make a shirt for her husband, and for this she gave me a piece of bear. Another asked me to knit a pair of stockings, for which she gave me a quart of peas. I boiled the peas and bear together and invited my owner and his mistress to dinner. She was filled with so much pride that she would not eat any of it because I had served them both in one dish.

I heard that my son had come to this village, so I went to see him. I found him lying on the ground, and I asked him how he could sleep like that. He replied that he was praying, and he lay down in this fashion so the Indians would not see what he was doing. I pray to God that my son will remember these things now that he has returned safely.

In this village, with the sun shining so hot and bright and with the smoke pouring from the huts, I could hardly distinguish one hut from another. In our village there was another captive who gave me a hat to wear. But her mistress came after me and snatched the hat away. One Indian woman gave me one spoonful of meal, and I put in my pocket for safekeeping. Even so, someone stole the meal and put five kernels of Indian corn in its place. This corn was the only provision I had in my travel for one day.

The Indians who returned from Northampton brought some horses and sheep with them. I asked them if they would carry me to Albany on one of their horses and sell me for gunpowder. I had no hope of getting home on foot the way that I had come. I could hardly bear to think of the many weary steps that I had taken to get to this place.

THE NINTH REMOVE

Instead of going either to Albany or toward home, we went five miles up the river and then crossed over. We stayed here awhile. In this place there lived a despicable Indian. He asked me to make him a shirt, and when I had finished, he refused to pay me for it. He lived by the riverside, and I often went to fetch his water for him. When I did this, I would remind him that he owed me money for my tasks. Finally he said that if I would make a shirt for his soon-to-be-born baby that he would give me a knife. When I finished this shirt, he did indeed give me the knife he had promised. When I went to my hut, my owner asked me to give him the knife. I was pleased to give it to him, for I was happy when I had anything I could give them that they would accept from me. His mistress had been gone three weeks, for she was getting corn from another Indian community. She brought about a peck and a half of corn home with her. During these days, the captain of this Indian party, Naananto, was killed.

Since my son now lived about a mile away from me, I asked if I could go and visit him. My captors allowed me to go, but I quickly got lost and could not find my way to him. I can't help marveling over God's wonderful power and goodness toward me, for though I encountered no Christian soul and met many Indians, I was never harmed. I had started back toward my village when I met my owner, and he showed me the way to my son. When I got to his village, I discovered that he was sick. He had a boil on his side, which bothered him very much. We cried together for a while over our sorrowful state, and I then returned to my village. Upon my return, I was no more satisfied than I had been before. I paced about, crying and complaining. My spirit sank low as I thought about my children. My son was ill, and I could only remember his sorrowful looks. He had no Christian friend near him who could help him either physically or spiritually. And I had no idea where my poor daughter was. I didn't know if she was sick or well, alive or dead. With such thoughts I pulled out my Bible (my great comforter in that time) and this scripture came to my hand: *Cast your burden on the LORD, and he will sustain you* (Ps. 55:22).

I wanted to find something to satisfy my hunger, so I looked among the huts and found a kind woman who gave me a piece of bear. I put it in my pocket and went to my hut. I could not find a way to cook it, though, for I was afraid that the Indians might find a way to steal it from me. So it lay in my pocket all day and night. I went back to the woman who had given it to me and asked her if she would let me boil the meat in the same pot in which she was boiling peanuts. She let me boil the meat in her pot, and she gave me some peanuts to eat with it. I cannot tell you how pleasant this meal was. I have noticed that the English sometimes bake bear meat, but the thought that it was bear meat made me shake. Now, though, such meat was very tasty to me.

One very bitterly cold day I could find no room to sit in front of the fire. I went into another hut where the woman placed a skin on the ground for me and asked me to sit down in front of their fire. She shared some peanuts with me and asked me to visit them again. She even said that they would buy me if they could. These were strangers that I had never talked with before.

THE TENTH REMOVE

On that day a small part of the Indian band moved about three-quarters of a mile away, intending to move farther away the next day. I was taken with this small band. Since I was hungry, I went back to the hut of the woman who had showed me such kindness. She told me to come in again. While I was there one of the Indians in the small party came looking for me. When he found me, he made me return to the small band of Indians, kicking me all the way. When I got back to this company, I discovered that they were roasting venison. They would not give me one bite of it to eat. Sometimes the Indians were nice to me, and at other times they were unpleasant.

THE ELEVENTH REMOVE

The next morning we began our journey up the river. I carried my load on my back. We soon came to a river that we waded over, and we climbed over steep hills. One hill was so steep that I had to crawl up it on my knees and hold onto the twigs and bushes to keep from falling backwards. I was also lightheaded and dizzy, but I hope all those weary steps I have taken simply take me one step closer to heavenly rest. *I know, O LORD, that your judgments are right, and that in faithfulness you have humbled me* (Ps. 119:75).

THE TWELFTH REMOVE

On the Sabbath morning, the Indians prepared for more travel. This morning I asked my owner if he would sell me to my husband, and he said, "Yes." I rejoiced in spirit over his answer. Before we went, my mistress had gone to a baby's burial. When she returned, I was sitting and reading my Bible. She grabbed it from my hands and threw it out of the hut. I ran out and picked it up, putting it in my pocket, and I never let her see it after that day. They then packed their things and gave me my load to carry. When I complained that it was too heavy, my mistress slapped my face and told me to start moving. I prayed to God, hoping that redemption would soon come, because their insolence grew worse and worse.

I was much cheered, though, by the thoughts of my going home. These thoughts made my burden seem light. However, I was soon disappointed when after traveling only a short distance, my mistress said she would not go any farther. She told me that I would have to return with her. She tried to persuade her husband to come back with us, but he would not, saying that he would return to us in three days. I was furious and very impatient with this decision. I could have died as easily as I could have returned. But I had to return. As soon as I could, I got out my Bible to read and this quieting scripture came to my hand, *Be still, and know that I am God!* (Ps. 46:10). Although these words calmed my spirit for a while, I knew that I still had some trials to go through. My owner was the best friend I had among the Indians, both in cold and hunger, and this quickly became apparent.

I tried to sit down, but my heart was full of sorrow over my plight, and I could not be still. Walking among the trees, I gathered some acorns and chestnuts, and these refreshed me a little bit. Toward night I gathered some sticks for my bed so that I wouldn't have to lie on the ground. But when I tried to lie down in the hut, they told me to find another place to sleep because they did not have enough room for me. I told them that I did not know where to go, but they told me to find some other place. When I continued to resist and complain, one of them pulled his sword and told me he would kill me if I did not leave. Thus I bent to the wishes of this rude man and went out into the night, even though I didn't know where I would go.

I went to one hut, and they told me that they had no room. Then I went to another, and they told me the same thing. Finally, an old Indian invited me to come into his hut, and his wife gave me some peanuts. She also gave me something on which I could lay my head, and we had a comfortable fire. Because of God's great providence I had comfortable lodging for that night. The next morning another Indian invited me to come that night and he would give me some peanuts, which he did.

In this place we were only about two miles from the Connecticut River. In the mornings we went out to gather peanuts, and we returned to the village at night. Every day I carried a huge load on my back, for they took everything everywhere they went. I told them the skin had rubbed completely off my back, but they offered no comforting answer. They replied only that it would not matter to them if my head had come off as well.

THE THIRTEENTH REMOVE

Instead of going to toward the Bay, which is what I wanted to do, I had to accompany them five or six miles down river into an overgrown thicket, where we camped for almost two weeks. While we were here, one woman asked me to make a shirt for her baby. In payment she gave me a large bowl of broth, which she thickened with meal made from tree bark. She added a handful of peas and some peanuts to the broth. I had not seen my son for a good while, and there was an Indian here whom I could ask about my son. The Indian told me that his owner had roasted my son and that he was very good meat indeed. The Indian himself claimed to have eaten a large piece of my son. The Lord boosted my spirit even in the face of such news. I recalled these Indians' horrible habit of lying and remembered that they do not know of a conscience that instructs them to tell the truth.

As I lay by the fire on this cold night, I took away a log that was keeping the fire's heat from me. An Indian woman moved the log down again. When I looked up at her, she threw a handful of ashes in my eyes. I thought I would be blind for the rest of my life, but since I was lying down, the water ran out of my eyes, carrying the ashes with it. By the next morning I had recovered my sight again. On occasions like this one, though, I hope it is not too much to say with Job, *Have pity on me, have pity on me, O you my friends, for the hand of God has touched me!* (Job 19:21). I can recall many times that I sat in the Indians' huts and suddenly leapt up and ran out, as if I had been at home, forgetting I was a captive in the wilderness. When I was outside the hut, I saw nothing but wilderness, woods, and a company of Indians. I quickly remembered where I was and thought of Samson, who said, *I will go out as at other times, and shake myself free* (Judges 16:20).

About this time, I started to think that all my hopes of being restored to my husband would not amount to anything. I hoped that the English army would come, but they never did. I hoped to be carried to Albany, as the Indians had talked about, but that never happened either. I thought of being sold to my husband, as my owner had promised, but my owner was now gone and I was left behind. My spirit had now sunk to its lowest state. I asked the Indians if I could go out and gather some sticks. This way I could be alone and pour my heart out to the Lord. I took my Bible with me to read, but I could find no comfort in it. I can say that even in all my sorrow God did not allow me to question the righteousness of his ways. I knew he had laid less on me than I deserved. A little while later, before this sorrowful time ended, the Lord showed me some scriptures that revived me a little bit: *For my thoughts are not your thoughts, nor are your ways my ways, says the* LORD (Is. 55:8). Also, *Commit your way to the* LORD; *trust in him, and he will act* (Ps. 37:5).

About this time some Indians came yelling and whooping from a raid on another village. They had killed three Englishmen there and had brought one captive with them. They surrounded this poor man, asking him many questions. I went out to see him, and when I came to him he was crying bitterly because he thought the Indians were going to kill him quickly. So I asked one of the Indians if they intended to kill the man, and he told me they would not. The captive was happy to hear such good news. I then asked him about my husband's welfare. The new captive told me that my husband was well but a little sad. I then knew that whatever the Indians had told me about him were nothing but lies. Some of them had told me that he was dead and they had killed him. Some had said he was married again because the governor had wanted him to marry again. The Indians had said that the governor told my husband that he should chose any woman he wanted as his wife, since I was dead.

While I was sitting in my hut, Philip's maid came in and asked me to give her a piece of my apron so she could make a blanket for her child. I told her I would not give this to her. My mistress then told me to give her my apron, and I still refused to do so. The maid told me that if I would not give her a piece of my apron that she would tear a piece of it off herself. I told her I would tear her coat if she did that. Then my mistress stood up, picked up a stick large enough to kill me, and tried to hit me with it. I stepped out of the hut and the stick stuck in the wall of the hut. While she was pulling the stick out, I ran to the maid and gave her my apron. So that storm blew over.

I heard that my son had come to this village, so I went to visit him. I told him that his father was well, but a little sad. My son told me he felt as sorry for his father as he did for himself. His talk struck me as a little strange, for I was burdened enough about myself to make me mindless of my husband and everyone else, since they were safe among their friends. He also told me that a few days before, his owner and some other Indians had been traveling to the French to trade him for some gunpowder when they met a band of Mohawk Indians. The Mohawks killed four Indians in my son's company, so the rest turned back and went home. This event is a blessing from the Lord, for his situation could have been worse if he had been sold to the French for gunpowder than it now was with the Indians.

I went to visit another English captive. I found him lying outside on the ground and asked him how he was doing. He told me he was suffering from dysentery because he was eating food that had so much blood in it. The Indians had thrown him out of their hut along with a baby, who was almost dead, on a bitterly cold day, without fire or clothes. This sight was enough to melt a heart of stone. They lay shivering in the cold. The young man was curled up like a dog, and the baby was stretched out with his eyes, nose, and mouth full of dirt, groaning but still alive. I advised the young man to find some fire. He told me he could not stand, but I persuaded him to move unless he wanted to lie there and die. With such urging I was able to get him to a fire, and I went home myself. As soon as I got home, my owner's daughter wanted to know what I had done with the English youth. I had to pray Paul's prayer, *that we may be rescued from wicked and evil people* (2 Thess. 3:2). In order to show her how he was doing, I took her to him. But before I got back home, it was rumored that I was running away and taking the English youth along with me. As soon as I walked through the door, they began to rant and rave, asking me where I had been and what I had been doing. While they were screaming that they were going to knock me out, I told them that I had been helping the English youth and that I was not planning to run away. They told me I was a liar, and picking up a hatchet they told me they would knock me out if I went outside again. They then confined me to the hut. Now I can say with David that *I am in great distress* (2 Sam. 24:14). If I stay in the hut, I will die from hunger; and if I go out, I will be killed.

I remained in distress for the next day and a half. Then the Lord, whose mercies are great, remembered me. An Indian came to me to ask if I could knit him a new pair of stockings. I told him he had to ask my mistress if I could go with him and do this for him. She said I could go, and I felt refreshed by the news. I had my freedom again. Then I went along with him and he gave me some roasted peanuts, which filled my rumbling stomach.

When I was out of her sight, I could pick up my Bible and read it again. My Bible was my guide by day and my pillow at night. Now I read a comforting scripture: *For a brief moment I abandoned you, but with great compassion I will gather you* (Is. 54:7). Thus the Lord carried me along from one time to another and made good this precious promise and many others. Then my son came to see me, and I asked his owner to let him stay awhile with me. When I combed his hair, I saw that his head was full of lice. He also told me, when I had finished combing his hair, that he was very hungry. I had nothing I could give him to relieve his hunger, but told him to stop into the huts he passed along the way to see if he could get any food from them. He did as I told him, but it seems he took too long to get home, for his owner was angry with him, beat him, and then sold him. My son then came running to tell me he had a new owner, who had already given him some peanuts. I went along with him to his new owner, who told me he loved my son and that my son would not lack anything. So this new owner carried him away, and I did not see my son again for a long while.

That night they made me go out of the hut once more. My mistress's baby was sick, and it died that night. The one benefit of this baby's death was that there was now more room in the hut. I went to another hut, and they invited me to come in and gave me a skin to lie down on as well as a dish of venison and peanuts. The next morning they buried the baby, and every morning and evening after that a company of women came to mourn with my mistress. I could not offer much condolence to them. I had many sorrowful days in this place, and I was often alone. *Like a swallow or crane I clamor, I moan like a dove. My eyes are weary with looking upward. O LORD, I am oppressed; be my security!* (Is. 38:14). I could tell the Lord, as Hezekiah did: *Remember now, O LORD, I implore you, how I have walked before you in faithfulness with a whole heart, and have done what is good in your sight* (Is. 38:3). Now I had time to examine all my ways. My conscience did not accuse me of any unrighteousness toward anyone, but I saw that in my walk with God I had been a careless creature. As David said, *Against you, you alone, have I sinned* (Ps. 51:4). And I might say with the Publican, *God, be merciful to me, a sinner!* (Luke 18:13). On the Sabbath days I could look at the sun and think about how people were going to the house of God to refresh their souls. They would then go to their homes to rest their bodies from their daily labors. But I was bereft of both of these things and could say like the poor Prodigal Son, *He would gladly have filled himself with the pods that the pigs were eating, and no one gave him anything* (Luke 15:16). For I must say with him, *Father, I have sinned against heaven and before you* (Luke 15:21). I recalled how on the night before and after the Sabbath my family, relatives, friends, and I would pray and sing and then refresh our bodies with God's good created things and be able to lie down on a comfortable bed. Instead of all this, I now had only a little swill for the body and like a pig had to sleep on the ground. I cannot tell you how much sorrow I felt. Only the Lord knows how sorrowful I was. In these times I would often recall that comforting scripture, *For a brief moment I abandoned you, but with great compassion I will gather you* (Is. 54:7).

THE FOURTEENTH REMOVE

Now we had to pack up and move on again. We left the thicket where we had been camping and moved on toward the towns on the Bay. I didn't have much to eat on this day. All I had were a few crumbs of cake that an Indian had given to my daughter on the day we were captured. I had kept it in my pocket since that day, and the crumbs were so hard and dry they were like little pebbles. But these refreshed me many times during the day when I was ready to faint from hunger. When I put these crumbs into my mouth I thought that if I ever returned to the colonies that I would tell the world how the Lord blessed such coarse food.

As we journeyed along, the Indians killed a pregnant deer. They gave me a piece of the fawn. The meat was so young and tender that I could eat the bones as well as the meat, and it tasted very good. That night it rained, but they built a hut of bark, and I stayed dry all night. When I got up in the morning I saw that many of the Indians had spent the night in the rain; I could tell by their smell. Thus the Lord dealt mercifully with me many times, and I fared better than many of them. In the morning they boiled the deer's blood in the deer's stomach. They offered me some of this food, but I could not eat it, even though the Indians thought it a delicacy. They were particular about other things, though. When I carried some water in a kettle and dipped my water dish into the kettle, they said they would knock me down if I did that again. They called me a dirty woman for dipping my water dish into the kettle.

THE FIFTEENTH REMOVE

So we kept on moving. I had a handful of peanuts to eat through that day. I carried my heavy load again that day, but I was looking forward to seeing home so much that I felt light-hearted. Sometimes one of the Indians would give me a pipe, another a little tobacco, and another a little bit of salt. I traded all these for some food. I cannot help thinking about the wolfish appetites that starving people have. Many times they gave me some hot food, and I devoured it greedily, burning my mouth. Even though my mouth hurt for hours afterward, I know I would do the same thing again. Sometimes I ate until I could eat no more, but I was as unsatisfied then as when I had begun my meal. Now I could understand that scripture, *You shall eat but not be satisfied* (Micah 6:14). I learned during my captivity that there are many scriptures that we do not notice or understand until we are troubled.

Now I could see more than ever before the miseries that sin had brought on us. Many times I would be ready to seek revenge against the Indians or to run away from them. But then I remembered a scripture that calmed my heart: *Does disaster befall a city, unless the* LORD *has done it?* (Amos 3:6). I pray that the Lord will help me to understand his word so that I can learn a lesson from it. *He has told you, O mortal, what is good; and what does the* LORD *require of you but to do justice, and to love kindness, and to walk humbly with your God?* (Micah 6:8–9).

THE SIXTEENTH REMOVE

We began our journey by wading across the Baquaug River. The water was up to our knees, and the current was swift. The water was so cold that I thought it would cut me in half. I was so weak that I walked unsteadily. I thought I would die here at last after getting through so many difficulties already. The Indians laughed to see me staggering along, but even in my distress the Lord helped me to experience the truth and goodness of his promise: *When you pass through the waters, I will be with you; and through the rivers, they shall not overwhelm you* (Is. 43:2). When I got across the river, I sat down and put on my stockings and shoes. I was crying so hard that the tears were running down my cheeks, and my heart was full of sorrow. But still I got up to go along with them.

Suddenly there appeared before us an Indian who told them that I must go to Wachuset to my owner. A letter from the Massachusetts Council about redeeming the captives had been delivered to the Indians there, and another letter would come in fourteen days. So I had to go there to be ready. Up until now, my heart had been so heavy that I could hardly speak. Now it was so light that I could run along the path. I regained my strength, and my knees and aching heart were now strong. Yet, the Indians traveled only one mile that night and then stayed in one place for the next two days. During those two days a company of about thirty Indians rode up to our camp. At first, my heart leapt for joy because I thought they were Englishmen. They were dressed in English clothing, with hats, white cravats, sashes around their waists, and ribbons on their shoulders. When they got nearer, though, I saw that there was a vast difference between the lovely faces of Christians and the foul looks of those men. My spirits sank low again.

THE SEVENTEENTH REMOVE

Because I was so hopeful, this part of the journey was comfortable. They gave me my pack, and we walked along cheerfully. But my will proved to be stronger than my body. Since I had little or no food, my strength failed me and my spirits sank very low. Now I can say with David: *For I am poor and needy, and my heart is pierced within me. I am like a shadow at evening; I am shaken off like a locust. My knees are weak through fasting; my body has become gaunt* (Ps. 109: 22–24).

That night we came to an Indian town, and the Indians sat down and were talking with one another about various matters. I was so tired I could hardly speak. So I went into one of the huts and found an Indian boiling some horses' feet. I asked the Indian for a little of the broth, and he took a dish and gave me some broth and a spoonful of porridge. I mixed some of the hot broth with the porridge and drank it and my spirits revived. The Indian also gave me a bit of small intestines, and I broiled them on the coals. Now I can say with Jonathan: *See how my eyes have brightened because I tasted a little of this honey* (1 Sam. 14:29). Now my spirit was revived again. The means of this restoration were poor and sparse, but the Lord bestowed his blessing on them, and they refreshed my body and soul.

THE EIGHTEENTH REMOVE

We picked up our packs and started walking again. I had a weary day, though. As we walked along, I saw an Englishman stripped naked and lying dead on the ground. Then we came to another Indian town, where we spent the night. There were four English captives in this town; one of them was my own sister. I went to visit her and to see how she was doing. She said she was well, considering her captive condition. I would have stayed with her that night, but the Indians who owned her would not allow me to do so. Then I went to another hut and there they were boiling some corn and beans. It smelled wonderful, but they would not let me eat any of it. Then I went into another hut, and in it I found two English children who were captives. The Indian woman was boiling horse feet, and she cut me off a little piece and gave a piece to one of the children. I ate mine quickly because I was so hungry. The child gnawed and sucked on its piece since it was so tough. Then I grabbed the child's piece and ate it myself, and it tasted very pleasant.

So I could now say with Job: *My appetite refuses to touch them; they are like food that is loathsome to me* (Job 6:7). The food that at other times I would have detested the Lord made pleasant tasting and refreshing. When I returned to my mistress's hut, she told me that I had disgraced them with my begging. If I begged any more they would kill me, she said. I replied that they could just as well kill me with a hatchet as to starve me to death.

THE NINETEENTH REMOVE

In the morning the Indians said that we would travel to Wachuset on that day. My day was bitter and weary, though, because I had been traveling for three days without rest. At last I saw the Wachuset hills, but they were many miles away. We came to a huge swamp, and we walked through it, up to our knees in the mud and water. I was so exhausted that I thought that I would have just given up here. But *when I thought, "My foot is slipping," your steadfast love, O LORD, held me up* (Ps. 94:18).

As I walked along, I held onto life, but I was spiritually weak. Just then one of the Indians came up to me and told me that in two more weeks I would see my husband. I asked if him if this was really true, and he replied that it was. Also, he said, you will come to your owner again, who had been away for three weeks. When we got to Wachuset, I met my owner again, and I was happy to see him. He asked me when I had last bathed, and I told him that it had been at least a month. He brought me some water himself and invited me to wash myself, and he gave me a mirror to see how I looked. He told his wife to give me something to eat, and she gave me a huge dish of beans and meat and some peanut-cake. My body and spirit were revived when they showed me such kindness. *He caused them to be pitied by all who held them captive* (Ps. 106:46).

My owner had three wives, and he lived sometimes with one and sometimes with another. One was this older woman in whose hut I now rested, and with whom he had spent these last three weeks. Another was the woman I had lived with and served while he was away. Her name was Wettimore. She was a proud person who liked to dress like a rich woman, with earrings and bracelets. She worked making belts of money and beads. The third woman was younger, and she had two babies. When I had received refreshment from the older mistress, Wettimore's maid came and called me back to Wettimore's hut. I began crying when I saw her, but the older mistress told me to come and see her again if I wanted any food. I returned with the maid, and for the first time Wettimore showed me some kindness. She laid down a mat for me to sleep on, and threw a rug over me to keep me warm. I then understood that if she let me go to serve the older mistress that she would lose both my service and the pay she would receive for my redemption. I was happy to hear this because it raised my hope that in God's due time this sorrowful situation would come to an end. Then an Indian came to me and asked me to knit him three pairs of stockings; for this he gave me a hat and a silk handkerchief. Another asked me to make her a dress, for which she gave me an apron.

Then two Indians brought the second letter from the Council about the captives. I burst into tears, and my heart was so full I could hardly speak. When I recovered my senses, I grabbed their hands and asked them how my husband and all my friends were doing. They said all these people were doing well, but were very sad. The Indians brought me two biscuits and a pound of tobacco. The tobacco I gave away quickly. When it was all gone, an Indian came up and asked me for some tobacco for his pipe. When I told him I did not have any more, he began to rant and rave. I told him that my husband would give him some tobacco when he came, but the Indian said that he would knock my husband's brains out if he came to this place. In the same breath he said that if one hundred men without guns came, the Indians would not harm them. These people were unstable and like madmen. Fearing the worst, I dared not send for my husband, even though there had been some talk about his coming to redeem me and take me home. I could not trust these Indians.

When the letter from the Council came, the Indians met to talk about the captives. They asked me how much my husband would pay to redeem me. This put me in quite a predicament, for as far as I knew all we owned had been destroyed in the Indian attack. If I suggested that my husband could pay only a little bit, the Indians might feel slighted. If I suggested a large amount, I was not sure where my husband might get the money. Finally, I suggested twenty pounds—a very large ransom—but I pleaded with them to take less. They would not hear of taking less, and they sent a message to Boston that I could be redeemed for twenty pounds. A Christian Indian wrote their letter for them.

Another Christian Indian told me he had a brother who would not eat horse because he had a scrupulous conscience. This Indian read his brother the scripture: *As the siege continued, famine in Samaria became so great that a donkey's head was sold for eighty shekels of silver* (2 Kings 6:25). The Indian explained this verse to his brother, and now he says that his brother will eat horse any time with any Indian. Another Christian Indian betrayed his own father, turning his father over to the English in order to save his own life. Another Christian Indian was so wicked and cruel that he wore a necklace of Christian fingers around his neck.

When my owner came home, he asked me to make a shirt for his baby. About the same time an Indian came to me and invited me to come to his hut that night to give me some pork and peanuts. As I was eating, another Indian said to me that though he seems to be your good friend, he killed two Englishmen at Sudbury. Their clothes are lying behind you. I looked around and saw bloody clothes with bullet holes in them, but the Lord protected me, and this Indian never did me any harm. Instead of hurting me, he gave me food many times; he and his wife provided food for me five or six times. If I went to their hut any time, they would always give me something, and yet they were strangers that I had never seen before. Another woman gave me a piece of fresh pork with a little salt in it, and she let me use her frying pan as well. I can't help remembering how sweet and pleasant this morsel was, for when we have food all around us, we rarely give full thanks for it.

THE TWENTIETH REMOVE

The Indians usually left one place when they had created some havoc, for they didn't want their deeds to be discovered. We went about three or four miles, and they built a hut large enough to hold at least one hundred Indians in preparation for a day of dancing and celebration. They talked a lot among themselves about whether the governor would send more information about the captives, for they thought he might be angry because of their attacks on certain towns. Such talk upset me a great deal. My sister was in a village not very far away from us. So she asked her owner if she could visit me. He gave her permission, and said he would go with her. Since she was ready before he was, she told him she would start the journey toward my settlement. She got about a mile or so away from my village when her owner caught up with her. He was so angry that he made her walk back in the rain to his village, so I never got to see her until we were in Charlestown. However, the Lord punished this man's actions, for he was hanged in Boston.

Many Indians now began to gather from all over the place in anticipation of the great day of celebration and dancing. Among the Indians was an English woman captive with whom I could share my feelings. I told her that my heart was so full of sorrow that it was ready to break. "I feel the same way," she said, "but I hope that very soon we shall hear some good news." I knew how much my sister and I wanted to see each other, but neither of us could get the chance to do so. I had not seen her since we had been taken captive. My daughter, whom I had not seen in about nine or ten weeks, was just about a mile away from me. I wanted to see my daughter so much that I begged them to let me go. The Indians were so hard-hearted that they would not let me go to see her. They used their tyrannical power while they could, but thanks to the Lord's wonderful mercy they did not have much time to wield this power.

On the Sabbath day, about seven in the morning, Mr. Hoar came from the Council with a third letter. My tribe called me into the hut when these three approached and told me to sit down and not to move. All of a sudden, my Indian guards grabbed their guns and ran off, as if the enemy were chasing them. I then heard some guns being fired. I looked very troubled, and the Indians asked me what was wrong. I told them I was afraid they had killed the Englishman, but they told me that they had fired over his horse, as warning shots, to show their power. They then allowed Mr. Hoar to come to their huts. I asked them to let me see him, but they refused. I was willing to wait until they permitted me to see him. When they had finished talking to him, they let me go to see him. We talked for a while, and I asked him if he was all right, and he asked me how I was doing. I asked him how my husband and friends were doing, and he told me that they were all well and would be happy to see me. My husband had sent me some things, including a pound of tobacco. I was able to sell it for nine shillings because the Indians wanted tobacco so much that they were now smoking hemlock and ivy to satisfy their desires.

I asked the Indians if I would go home with Mr. Hoar. They told me no, so I went to bed with that answer. In the morning, Mr. Hoar invited the Indians to dinner, but then he found that overnight they had stolen the greatest part of his provisions from his bags. God's wonderful power had protected us in the night. There were so many hungry Indians who wanted a little good food that they could have killed us to get it. But instead of doing us any harm, they seemed to be ashamed of the theft, and they blamed another group of Indians for it. We then could see that no task is too hard for God. God showed his power over the Indians in this situation, just as he did over the hungry lions when Daniel was cast into the lions' den.

That night, in the midst of all their celebrations, I asked them if I would be able to go home. They all said that I would not be able to go home until my husband came to get me. When Mr. Hoar and I went to bed that night, my owner left the hut. In a little while another Indian came in and told Mr. Hoar that my owner would let me go home tomorrow if Mr. Hoar would let my owner have a pint of liquor. Mr. Hoar asked his own Indian guides to accompany this Indian and have my owner swear to it in front of all three of them. When my owner made his oath, Mr. Hoar gave him the liquor. Then another Indian, seeing what my owner was up to, asked me what I would give him to say a good word for me so I could go home tomorrow. I told him I would give him anything I had, and asked him what he wanted. He told me he would like two coats, twenty shillings, half a bushel of seed-corn, and some tobacco. I thanked him for his concern, but I knew that I didn't need his help, since I already knew I was going home. My owner, who had been drinking a great deal, came into the hut and proposed a drink to Mr. Hoar's health one moment and a drink to his death the next. He said over and over that Mr. Hoar should be hanged. Then he called for me, and I was afraid of what he might say to me. But he was very civil to me. He was the first Indian that I saw drunk during my entire captivity. He eventually left to spend the night with one of his wives, so he did not trouble us any that night.

Yet, I did not rest comfortably that night. I did not sleep for three nights. I had not rested the night before the letter came from the Council because I was so afraid. God often leaves us in the dark when our deliverance is close at hand. I could not rest during the day or night before the letter came. On the day Mr. Hoar came with such good news I was overjoyed. The third night I was consumed with so many thoughts: Would I ever go home again? Must I go home and leave my children in the wilderness and never see them again? I could not sleep at all thinking about these things.

On Tuesday morning the Indians met in their general court to decide whether I should go home. Almost unanimously they agreed that I should be able to go home.

Before I continue my story, I want to mention a few remarkable examples of God's providence that I witnessed during my captivity.

1.   It is remarkable that our English army got so near in their pursuit of the Indians that the army nearly captured them. The Indians were so hungry that the soldiers could have followed their trails by tracking the Indians' desperate diggings for roots to eat. What is stranger is that our army would suddenly run out of its provisions and have to give up the chase and return to their fort. The very next week the Indians attacked our town like so many ravenous wolves that tore our lambs and us to death. God seemed to leave his people to fend for themselves, and ordered all things for his holy ends. *Does disaster befall a city unless the* LORD *has done it? They are not grieved over the ruin of Joseph! Therefore they shall now be the first to go into exile, and the revelry of the loungers shall pass away. This is the* LORD'S *doing; it is marvelous in our eyes* (Amos 3:6; 6:6–7; Ps. 118:23).

2. I can remember how the Indians derided the English army's slowness in setting out after us. As I went along with the Indians, they asked me when I thought the army might begin chasing us. I told them I had no idea, and they made fun of the army, saying it would probably be six months before they came after us.

3. Eventually the English army did begin to pursue us. When the Indians realized this, they began to move from camp to camp. When we came to the Baquaug River, the Indians crossed over safely, but the army was not able to cross the river. I have to admire God's wonderful providence in preserving the Indians to bring more woe on our country. The Indians could cross the river in great numbers, but the English had to stop. God had a hand in all of this.

4. The English thought that if they destroyed the Indians' corn, the Indians would starve and die. So the English destroyed the corn and drove the Indians into the woods in the midst of winter. Yet the Lord strangely provided for the Indians so that I did not see one Indian starve during my captivity. Many times the Indians would eat food that not even a hog or a dog would touch. With such nourishment God gave them strength to be a scourge to his people. The Indians usually ate nuts and acorns and several other weeds and roots whose names I did not know. They would pick up old bones and cut them into pieces. If the bones had maggots in them, they would boil the bones until the maggots crawled out. They would then use the bones to make soup. They would eat horse's guts and ears and all sorts of wild birds. They also ate bear, venison, beavers, tortoise, frogs, squirrels, dogs, skunks, rattlesnakes, and tree bark. They also ate whatever provisions they could steal from the English. The Indians would often

eat up all their food in the morning but still have some food to take care of their needs. I can't help admiring the wonderful power of God in providing for such a large number of our enemy in the wilderness. *O that my people would listen to me, that Israel would walk in my ways! Then I would quickly subdue their enemies, and turn my hand against their foes* (Ps. 81:13–14). Our perverse and evil activities have so offended the Lord that, instead of punishing our enemies, the Lord feeds and nourishes them so they can be a scourge to the whole land.

5. Yet when the Indians seemed to have reached a pinnacle of success and the English had so miserably failed, God providentially turned things around. The Indians held me captive for eleven weeks and five days. Not one week passed when they did not attack one village or another. They mourned their own losses, but they rejoiced in their cruelty to the English. They boasted very much about their victories, saying that they had done a good deed by sending the English to heaven so soon. They would brag that during the summer they would kill all the English or drive them back to England. The Indians began to think that they controlled the world, while the Christians began to despair. We captives lifted our eyes to God, praying sincerely, *Lord, save us! We are perishing!* (Mt. 8:25). When the Lord had brought his people so low, they finally realized that only the Lord could help them now. He now took the situation into his own hands. Although the Indians thought they had made a pit as deep as hell for the Christians, the Lord hurled the Indians into it. The Lord has just as many ways to destroy the Indians as he once had to preserve them.

Now to return to my story about going home: Here also providence was at work, for at first the Indians would not permit me to go home, but insisted that my husband had to come to get me. Soon, though, they agreed that I should go home, and many were very happy about this. Some of them asked me to send them bread, some asked for tobacco, others shook my hand and offered me clothes for the ride. Not one of them argued against my going home.

The Lord answered my prayers and the prayers of others. During my travels an Indian told me that he and his wife would run away with me and take me home. I told them that I was not willing to run away but that I would wait on God to take me home quietly and without fear. Now God has granted me my wishes. I have certainly seen God's wonderful power through all my experiences. I was in the midst of those roaring lions and savage bears night and day. None of them feared God or man or the devil. Yet not one of them raped me or sexually abused me. Some will say that I give myself credit for this, but I say this to glorify God. God's power is as great now as when he preserved Daniel in the lions' den or the three children in the fiery furnace. *O give thanks to the* LORD, *for he is good; for his steadfast love endures forever. Let the redeemed of the* LORD *say so, those he redeemed from trouble* (Ps. 107:1–2). I came out of the midst of so many hundreds of enemies and I was not harmed.

So I left the Indians, and along the way I started crying more fitfully than I ever had during my captivity. I couldn't believe I was actually going home now. Mr. Hoar, his Indian guides, and I came to Lancaster, and it was a somber sight to me. I had lived many comfortable years there with my family and friends. Now there was not one house left standing, nor was there anyone in sight. We traveled through the town to a farmhouse, where we spent the night. Even though straw was all we had for our beds, we still spent a comfortable night there. The Lord preserved us safely that night. He awakened us the next morning and carried us through the day until just before noon we came to Concord. I was full of joy, even though I had some sorrow, to see so many Christians together there. Some of them had been my neighbors. I met my brother and my brother-in-law there. The latter asked if I knew where his wife was. Poor soul, he had helped bury her and he did not remember it. She was shot down by the house and burned beyond recognition. Some of the townspeople who had retreated safely to Boston came back to Lancaster after the attack to bury the dead, and he could not recognize her body because it had been so badly burned. I was sorrowful to know how many were still captives, my children among them, and longing to enjoy the deliverance I had now received. I did not know if I would ever see them again.

We went to Boston that day where I met with my dear husband. However, we could not stop thinking about our children—one was dead, and we did not know where our other two were—and these thoughts kept us from taking full comfort in each other's arms. I had just been surrounded by merciless and cruel persons, but now I was surrounded by compassionate Christians. So many Christians took me into their houses that I cannot begin to tell you how much love I received from their hearts. Some of them I knew, and others I did not know, but the Lord knows them all by name, and I hope he will reward them seven-fold for all their goodness. Several women in Boston raised the twenty pounds that paid the price of my redemption. Mr. Shepherd of Charlestown took us into his house, and we lived there for eleven weeks. He and his wife were like a father and mother to my husband and me. We met many more tenderhearted friends there. We were now in the midst of love, even though our hearts were still full of sorrow for our children and friends who were still being help captive.

Not long after I was released, the Council sent another letter to the Indians, and they released my sister and another captive. Although we still did not know where our children were, we continued to hope that we would soon see them again. The memory of my dead child weighed more heavily on my mind than did the thoughts of my children who were still captives. I kept thinking how my child had suffered from her wounds, how I was unable to care for her properly, and how the Indians buried her in the wilderness, away from any Christians. We heard many reports about our children, some positive and some negative, but we still had no specific news about them.

About this time the Council ordered a day of public Thanksgiving. I didn't feel very thankful yet because I was still mourning. My husband and I decided we would ride to the east to see if we could get any information about our children. As we rode along between Ipswich and Rowley, we met a man who told us that our son, Joseph, had been bought by someone nearby, and that he himself had bought my sister's son. We traveled along until we came to Newbury, where the town wanted my husband to preach the Thanksgiving sermon, since their minister was not there. After he preached there, someone came in and told us that our daughter was in Providence. God has fulfilled that precious scripture that comforted me so much when I continued to mourn over my lost children. When my heart was so full of sorrow— because I did not know where my children were—and I was walking through the valley of the shadow of death, the Lord revived me with his word. *Thus says the* LORD: *Keep your voice from weeping, and your eyes from tears; for there is a reward for your work, says the* LORD: *they shall come back from the land of the enemy* (Jer. 31:16).

Now we were between our children, the one in the east and the other in the west. We went to see our son first, since he was in Portsmouth. We met with him and his owner, who told us that he could not redeem our son for less than seven pounds. The good people around there were happy to help us gather the money to pay the price. I pray that the Lord will reward this man and all those others, even though I did not know them, for their love and help. Now that we had found and recovered one of our children, we hurried to find the other one. As we traveled back though Newbury, my husband preached there, and they paid him well for his labors.

When we got to Charlestown we found that the governor of Rhode Island had sent for our daughter so that he could take care of her. Since she was nearer Delaware than Rhode Island, another Christian man took her to his house to take care of her. We marveled at God's goodness, especially in our poverty. He surrounded us with compassionate friends, even though we could not repay them for their love. The English army brought our daughter with them to Dorchester, where we met her safely. The Lord's power is great and he can do whatever seems good to him. The Lord has blessed us so much. Now I have seen that scripture fulfilled: *Even if you are exiled from the ends of the world, from there the LORD your God will gather you, and from there he will bring you back. The LORD your God will put all these curses on your enemies and the adversaries who took advantage of you* (Deut. 30:4, 7). Thus the Lord has brought us out of that horrible pit and has placed us in the midst of compassionate Christians. I hope with all my soul that we can continue to be worthy of the mercies that God has given us and that he continues to give us.

Now that our family was together once again, the South Church in Boston rented a house for us. We lived there for about nine months, and the Lord provided graciously for us. It seemed strange to start over again in a house with such bare walls. We were soon able to furnish the house, though, because of the benevolence of many Christian friends in the colonies and in England who provided money for us. The Lord has been so good to us that even when we did not have a house or other necessities he provided food, clothing, and shelter for us through the love of others. *A true friend sticks closer than one's nearest kin* (Prov. 18:24). We have now found such compassionate friends here and are happy to live among them.

I can recall the time that I used to sleep soundly without my thoughts so preoccupied. Things are different now. Now, when everyone around me is asleep, I think about the past and the events we endured. God carried us through our situation with wonderful power and strength, and he returned us safely and unharmed. I remember that I was once in the midst of darkness. I was surrounded by thousands of enemies and thought that I faced certain death. I had a hard time convincing myself that I would ever be able to eat with my family and friends again. Now we are fed with the finest of wheat and with honey out of the rock. As I think about God's love and goodness toward me, I believe that it is as true of me as of David, who said of himself: *I drench my couch with my weeping* (Ps. 6:6). I have seen and been so touched by God's wonderful power so that while others are sleeping, I am weeping.

I have seen how things in this world change so quickly. One moment I was healthy, wealthy, and lacking nothing, and the next moment I was sick, wounded, and near death, experiencing nothing but sorrow and hardship.

Before I knew what hardship really was, I was sometimes ready to pray for it. When I prospered, having the comforts of the world around me, I was cheerful. I saw many people who were experiencing trials and sorrows, and who were sick and poor. I was sometimes jealous because I wanted to have my portion of hardships in this life, and that scripture would often come to mind: *For the Lord disciplines those whom he loves* (Heb. 12:6). Now I see that the Lord acted in his own time and ways to discipline me. Some experience their hardships in drops, and one drop follows another. The Lord provided me a full cup of hardships. I wanted hardships and I got hardships in full measure. Even so, I have learned that when God calls us to carry any burden, he will carry us through the hardship and teach us certain lessons from the hardships. I hope I can say, as David did, *It is good for me that I was humbled* (Ps. 119:71). The Lord has taught me the vanity of all these material things. They are but a shadow and things that do not last. We must rely on God himself. Whenever small matters trouble me, I now have an experience that I can use to check my complaints. I can recall that it was not long ago that I would have given the world for my freedom or have gladly been a servant to a Christian. I have learned to look beyond present and smaller troubles and to endure them patiently. *Do not be afraid, stand firm, and see the deliverance that the LORD will accomplish for you today* (Ex. 14:13).

A NOTABLE EXPLOIT:
A HEROIC WOMAN FROM
MAGNALIA CHRISTI AMERICANA

Hannah Dustan

On March 15, 1697, Indians descended upon the outskirts of Haverhill, murdering and capturing about thirty-nine people and burning about six houses. Hannah Dustan was in bed with her one-week-old baby. Her nurse, Mary Neff, who was a widow, was with Hannah when a band of Indians came near the Dustans' house, intending to attack it and carry out their bloody deeds.

Hannah's husband hurried home, hoping to rescue his family. He instructed seven of his children—who ranged in age from two years old to seventeen years old—to run away as fast as they could to the protection of the town. He then went in to tell his wife that the Indians were attacking them. Before she could get up, the fierce Indians had come so close to the house that her husband did not think he could save his wife. So he ran after his children, resolving to carry those with him that he loved the most and leave the rest to God's care. When he caught up with his children, he could not declare that he loved any one more than another. So he decided to live or die with all of them. When a band of Indians overtook them, he stayed behind to hold off the Indians as his children marched on. Although the Indians fired several shots, they did not hit him or any of the children. Because of God's providence, he and his children arrived safely in a place about two miles away from his house.

His wife did not fare so well, however. The nurse tried to escape with the newborn infant, only to fall into the hands of the attackers. The Indians who came into the house told Hannah to get out of bed at once. Astonished, she arose and sat by the chimney, fearing for her life. The marauding Indians stole whatever they could carry away from the house and then set it on fire. About twenty Indians led these women away with about ten other English captives.

Before they had gone very far, the Indians dashed out the brains of the infant against a tree. Several of the other captives soon complained of being tired, and the Indians killed them by burying their hatchets in their brains and leaving their bodies on the ground for the birds and animals to eat. That night Hannah and her nurse traveled about twelve miles. Over the next few days they journeyed one hundred and fifty miles with the Indians who had captured them. Despite the hardships of their travel, including inadequate shelter and food, their health did not suffer in any noticeable ways.

These two women were now in the hands of people whose tender mercies were cruelties. Our good God, who holds all hearts in his own hands, heard these women's sighs and provided them unexpected favor from their new Indian owner. There were twelve people in the Indian family: two large men, three women, and seven children. These Indians had learned to pray from the French. The Indian family had converted to the Roman Catholicism that some French missionaries had taught them. So they prayed at least three times a day—in the morning, at noon, and in the evening. They would not let their children eat or sleep without saying their prayers. Even though these Indians prayed in this way, they would not allow Hannah and Mary to say their prayers, and they hindered these women whenever they could.

Even so, these poor women could make their lives comfortable and tolerable only by praying fervently. Since the Indians sent the women out to work, either together or apart, they did have the chance to do as the biblical Hannah did, and pour out their souls to God. Of course, their friends in our community also poured out their intercessory prayers for the women.

When their Indian owner saw that their spirits were down, he would say: "Why should you trouble yourselves? If God is going deliver you, you have nothing to worry about, for he will rescue you in due time." It does seem that our God willed to rescue them in his own time.

The Indian family, with these two women captives, left their place to journey to a meeting with some other Indians. They told the women that in this new place they would be stripped, whipped, and made to run the gauntlet through an entire army of Indians. They told the women that Indians usually welcomed captives in this way to a new town. The Indians ridiculed some of the faint-hearted English who passed out during the torments of this discipline.

On April 30, though, when they were about one hundred and fifty miles away from the Indian town, these women performed a heroic act of escape. While the Indians were sleeping peacefully, Hannah decided to act on the Indians as Jael had acted on Sisera. Since Hannah was in a place where no law ruled her life, she thought that law did not forbid her to kill her murderers, who had already butchered her baby. She encouraged Mary, the nurse, and another captive to help her with her plan. Grabbing some hatchets, they struck their Indian oppressors with such hard blows that before the Indians could get up to defend themselves they fell down dead. One badly wounded Indian woman escaped. One little boy, whom they had planned to take with them, woke up and ran away.

They scalped the ten Indians they had killed and received fifty pounds from the General Assembly of the province as a reward for their action. They also received many congratulatory presents from their friends as well as a very generous token of appreciation from the Governor.

GOD'S MERCY SURMOUNTING MAN'S CRUELTY, EXEMPLIFIED IN THE CAPTIVITY AND REDEMPTION OF

Elizabeth Hanson

*T*he providence of God toward his people is indeed remarkable. He has delivered them from many times of trouble. To help us remember his great providence we can always recall that marvelous truth that God is always near us and always ready to help those who place their faith in him and obey his commandments.

The Scriptures provide illustrations of God's providence in the stories of the Israelites, Job, David, Daniel, Paul, and Silas. Modern history also contains many examples of God's parental care of his people in their most difficult trials and deepest distresses. All of these stories from the Bible and from modern history remind us that God does not change but is the same yesterday, today, and tomorrow.

There are many modern stories of God's mercy and providence. One of them illustrates his goodness and his sustaining care of the faithful better than other stories. On August 27, 1724, some Indians captured Elizabeth Hanson and her four children and servant. She told this story to a friend, who wrote it down faithfully, almost word for word.

For several days many Indians were hiding in the fields near our town, waiting until my husband and the other men in the town had left. When they knew the men had gone, two Indians broke into our house, and then eleven more rushed in. They furiously attacked us with their tomahawks and guns. They killed one child immediately, intending to scare us as much as possible and make us afraid of them.

The leader of the Indians ran up to me and was going to kill me, but I pleaded with him to spare my life, and he did. Our servant and four of my six children were with me. My youngest child was just fourteen days old. I was not very fit for the hardships I had to endure, and that I describe in this account of my captivity.

The Indians ransacked our house, taking linens and whatever else they wanted for themselves. As soon as they had gathered everything they wanted, the Indians ran out of the house. Two of my younger children—aged six and four—who had been playing in the orchard, came into the yard about that time. When they saw the Indians, they cried out with surprise. One of the Indians ran over to them, grabbed one child under each arm, and carried them to us. My servant tried to calm the children so they wouldn't make so much noise. She was able to get my six-year-old to quiet down, but my four-year-old was so frightened that it would not stop crying. Because they did not want the child's cries to draw attention to them, the Indians brutally killed my four-year-old right before my eyes. I did the best I could not to scream out or to appear disturbed, for I did not want them to kill the other child in the same way. I wish that my children had never run into the yard but had kept out of sight until the Indians had taken us from our house.

When they had killed my two children, they scalped them. Scalping is a common practice with these Indians. Whenever they kill any English person, they cut the skin off from the crown of the head and carry it with them as evidence of their killing. Sometimes they even get paid a reward for every scalp. The Indians then got ready to leave the house in a hurry, not stealing anything other than what they had already gathered. They took these things, my little fourteen-day-old baby, my six-year-old son, my two daughters—one sixteen and the other fourteen—my servant, and me.

I was very weak, since I had been in bed since my baby's birth fourteen days earlier. I had lived in a nice room well supplied with a comfortable bed, a warm fire, and other things that allowed me a restful recovery from my labor and delivery. Having to leave these comforts in my condition made my hardships greater than they would have been if I had been stronger and healthier. But I could not resist the Indians; I had to go with them or they would have killed me.

So we left the house, and each Indian was carrying something. I carried my baby with me, and my three children walked along beside me. Although the Indians' leader was carrying a heavy load, he carried my baby for me. I took this to mean that he favored me some. We walked through several swamps, and the Indians avoided all roads or paths so their footsteps could not be tracked.

I guess we must have walked about ten miles from my house by that night. The Indians set up camp and lit a fire. Some of them slept while others guarded our camp. I was wet and tired, and I did not get much rest lying on the cold ground that night.

As soon as it was daylight, we had to start moving. We traveled very hard all day over many rivers, brooks, and swamps, because the Indians were avoiding the roads. At night I was very tired and wet and had to sleep again on the cold ground. We traveled like this for twenty-six days. Sometimes our travels took us over lakes and ponds. We also crossed some high mountains. Some of these mountains were so steep that I had to crawl up them on my hands and knees. At such times the Indian leader would often carry my baby for me. I took this as a sign of God's favor that this Indian gave me so much help and that he was so compassionately inclined to help me. Even though the leader had a heavy burden of his own, he always stood ready to help me and would often carry my blanket as well. Then I had nothing to carry, so that I could help my little boy. Sometimes I carried him in my arms because he was so small, and at other times he would help me climb up hard places in the mountains. This Indian leader showed more humanity and civility than I would have expected, so I secretly thanked God for being the cause of this great mystery and providence.

We also had to wade through some very deep brooks and other bodies of water. Sometimes we were up to our waists in the water, and sometimes our girls were up to their shoulders and chins. The Indians carried my son on their shoulders often when we were crossing such deep waters. When we sat down beside one of these bodies of water, the Indians often asked my oldest daughter, Sarah, to sing them a song. When they asked her to do this, she often thought of the words of the Psalm: *By the rivers of Babylon—there we sat down and there we wept when we remembered Zion. On the willows there we hung our harps. For there our captors asked us for songs, and our tormentors asked for mirth* (Ps. 137:1–3). I was very touched when my child told me this. I was very worried about her, but I was glad to hear that she remembered the biblical teachings. She wanted so much to have a Bible that we could read for spiritual comfort during these times of distress.

We also had to cross over and through thick swamps. My Indian leader would sometimes lead me by hand much of the way through these bogs. He gave me whatever help he could in these difficult times.

Our greatest hardship was lack of food. Many times we had nothing to eat but pieces of old beaver skin coat, which they used more for food than for clothing. They cut them into long strips and gave us little pieces. We laid them on the fire until all the hair had been singed off, and then we ate them as a sweet morsel, knowing that *to an ravenous appetite even the bitter is sweet* (Prov. 27:7).

Even though we did eat such unnourishing food, we had very little of it to eat. We never had much energy. My children's complaints, especially my little son's, added to my own troubles. Sometimes the Indians would catch a squirrel or a beaver, but at other times all we had to eat were nuts, berries, or roots. We didn't eat any corn for a long time. Some of the younger Indians stole some ears of corn from the field of an English farm, but they didn't give us very much of it. When they caught a beaver, we lived well while the meat lasted. The Indians allowed my children and me to eat the entrails and the other parts they didn't want. The Indians did not allow us to wash this food as it should have been washed, so the food was very repugnant to us. Nothing other than our desperate hunger could make this food appealing to us, but such hunger makes every bitter thing sweet.

Our daily travel and hard living caused my milk almost to dry up completely. This was one of my greatest difficulties. I fretted over how I could sustain my poor baby's life, and keeping her alive was always on my mind. Sometimes I had nothing but cold water to give to my baby. I would take the water in my mouth and let it fall on my nipple so that my baby could suck in the water with whatever she could get from my breast. Whenever I had any broth made from beaver or any beaver entrails, I fed these to my baby as well as I could. In this way, and keeping her as warm as I could, I was able to sustain her life until we got to Canada. There I was able to get some other food, and I will write about that later.

Having come so far, the Indians decided to split up. We had to be divided among them. This caused us a great deal of grief, but we had to do what they told us to do. There was no way we could help ourselves. They took my oldest daughter away from me first to a faraway part of the country. My heart broke when they took her away.

We did not travel very far after this before they split up again and took my second daughter and servant away from me into another part of the country. Now I had only my six-year-old boy and my baby with me. My daughter and servant experienced terrible hardships after we were separated. They traveled three days without food, with nothing but cold water to sustain them. After three days, my servant—who was tired, cold, hungry, and wet—fainted. The Indians treated her tenderly because they did not want her to die. They had come so near home that they hoped they could make more ransom on her if she lived.

In a few more days they were near the end of their journey. They then had plenty of corn and other food. They did not have much meat, though, and when their hunting trips were not successful, they did not have very many provisions. It was not long before my daughter and my servant were separated. My daughter's owner was sick and unable to hunt for meat, and they also had no corn in their camp. So they were forced to eat tree bark for an entire week.

This little group was starving, and some other Indians heard of their situation. These Indians came to visit my daughter and her owners and brought them a beaver's entrails and liver. These people are very kind and helpful to one another, which is very commendable. They made a good meal out of this meat, especially since there were only four of them: the Indian, his wife and daughter, and my daughter.

By now, my Indian owner and our little band had reached the end of our journey. We had better food here because we had some corn, venison, and wild fowl. My owner had a large family of fifteen, so sometimes we did not have enough food, especially when game was scarce.

Our shelter was still not much better here than when we were traveling through the woods. I still had to sleep on the cold ground, even though we slept inside a tent. The Indians can set up and take down these tents so easily that they often carry them from one place to another. Our clothing was thin, and our shoes and socks were worn out from our travels, so we did not have much protection from the cold. Because of our lack of warm socks, both my little boy's feet froze, as did one of mine and one of my little baby's. Although this was quite a challenge, we all did well thanks to God's mercy.

Even though we had reached the end of our journey, we never stayed in one place very long, moving from one place to another. They moved so much in order to hunt. Our lodging was more unpleasant than if we had stayed in one place. Even though we slept in the tents, the ground was still cold and damp and made for unhealthy sleeping.

Eventually we reached the Indian fort, and many Indians came to greet us and welcome my owner home. They held a great celebration with dancing, shooting guns, shouting, drinking, and eating. They celebrated to excess for several days, which I suppose was their way of giving thanks to God for their safe return and great success. While the Indians were celebrating, I lost myself in my own spiritual reflections. I prayed that with my dear children separated from me and with my hardships that I would not question God's purposes for my life. I also prayed that I could trust deeply in our God who rules the hearts of all people and can do what he pleases in the kingdoms of the earth. I know that he sustains those who place their faith in him and who trust him. I had a hard time resigning myself to God's power and strength, though, because I could not stop thinking about my trials. I was also so worried about my children that I could not fully submit myself to God's providence and mercy. I was so troubled that I cannot even describe how truly difficult my hardships were.

We had not been here very long before my owner went out on a hunting trip and was gone about a week. He ordered me to gather nuts and cut wood while he was gone. I diligently went out every day and cut and carried wood back to our tent.

When he returned, he was not very happy because he had not had much luck in killing any animals. So he took his revenge on us poor captives. He did allow my child and me to eat a little bit of boiled corn. Even so, he was so angry that he threw a stick or corncob at me with such violence that it seemed he held a grudge against us for eating. When he did this, his wife and daughter broke out crying and sobbing. I was afraid that trouble was brewing against us, so I immediately went out of his tent into another one. He chased furiously after me and tore my blanket off my back. He took my little boy away from me and hit him so that he knocked my son down to the ground. My son was not hurt, but he was frightened. He got up and ran away without crying. Then my Indian owner left me, but his wife's mother came and sat down by me and told me that I could sleep in her tent that night. She went away for a few minutes and came back with a small skin with which she covered my feet. She told me that my owner intended to kill us. I wanted to know why, for I had done everything he had asked me to do while he was out hunting. Even though we could not talk to each other, I let her know how unreasonable he was being. She then made a sign to me that I would indeed die and that I should pray to God and prepare for death. The poor old woman was very kind and tender, and she would not leave me that night. She lay down at my feet, planning to do what she could to assuage her son-in-law's anger, for he had planned to kill me mainly, as best as I could understand, because the lack of food caused him to do it. I didn't sleep much that night, even with my poor baby sleeping sweetly beside me.

I dreaded my owner's plan, and I woke up every hour expecting him to come and kill us. But he was so tired from his hunting and tromping in the woods that he forgot his plan and slept through the night. The next day he went out hunting again. I was afraid that his trip would again be unsuccessful, and I prayed that he would catch some food to satisfy his hunger and cool his anger. He was gone only a short time when he returned with some wild ducks he had shot. He ordered that the ducks be prepared as quickly as they could. When these Indians have plenty, they use it up as quickly as they get it, consuming in gluttony and drunken excess in two days as much as might last up to one week with careful management. During this plentiful time I felt the comfort of being well fed, for my owner sent a portion of the food to my little ones and me. My spirits brightened a little bit now since the bitterness of death had passed for now at least.

Not long after this, my owner got upset with me again and threatened to kill me. I noticed that whenever he felt like this that he lacked food and was hungry. Whenever he had successful hunting trips, he was in a better mood. For then he had plenty of food to eat, and his appetite was always satisfied. My owner naturally had a hot temper, though, and he often threw sticks, stones, or whatever he could find to throw whenever he was angry. My life was continually in danger. In his great providence, my God preserved me so that I was never hurt very badly. For this I want always to be thankful to my Maker.

When they did not have very much meat around, the Indians allowed us to eat only the intestines and other entrails. They allowed us only to clean the feces out of the intestines but we could not wash them. So we had to boil them in that filthy condition and eat them. Although this was unpleasant, our hunger made it easy for us to eat this food. This filthy food, which they gave us so often, became pretty tolerable to our fierce appetites, for otherwise we could have not eaten it. Nobody knows what he or she can endure until they undergo trials. What I would not have ever served my family because it was not fit for them was now a sweet morsel and a tasty dish.

By now, I was so exhausted from hard work, poor diet, and lack of sleep that I became very, very discouraged. In addition, my milk dried up so that my poor, weak baby looked just like a skeleton. I could feel her bones through the skin. I was at a loss to know how I could get some food to nourish my baby. Seeing my distress, one of the Indian women told me a way that I could provide some nourishment for my baby. She told me to clean some kernels from walnuts and beat them with a little bit of water. When I did this, the water looked like milk. Then she told me to add some cornmeal to the water and to boil all of this together for a little while. When I followed her instructions, I had made a meal that was both tasty and nourishing. After eating this food, my baby started to look better and to get stronger. I discovered that the Indians often nurse their infants on this diet.

I took great comfort that my baby was recovering. But my comfort was soon mixed with bitterness and trouble. When my Indian owner saw that my baby was again thriving, he said that when the baby grew fat enough he would kill her and eat her. When he thought the time was right, he grabbed a stick that he had prepared to use as a spit on which to roast the baby. He made me sit down beside him and undress my baby. When the child was naked, he felt her arms, legs, and thighs, and told me that she was not fat enough yet and that I should dress the baby again until she was ready.

I could not believe that my owner pretended that he wanted to harm my baby only to tease and aggravate me. I was so worried that I had a hard time believing that God would preserve our lives from the cruel hands of this Indian, even though I put my trust in God's overwhelming power night and day.

Shortly after this, my owner got sick. While he was lying sick in his tent, he ordered his son to beat my son. The Indian boy's grandmother intervened and would not allow her grandson to beat my son. Then my owner grabbed a very sharp stick and threw it very violently at my son, hitting him in the chest. The blow bruised my son, and the pain and surprise of the blow made him turn a deathly pale. I asked my son not to cry, and though he was only six years old, he endured this treatment with great patience. He did not complain, and his patience softened my owner's hard heart. My owner no doubt would have grown more passionate and resentful if my child had cried out, for my owner's anger always grew stronger when he heard complaining cries. Later the same day my owner got up and started walking around, but he was far from being well. His wife and daughter told me that my master intended to kill me even though he was sick. I was afraid of how things might end unless providence intervened. So I put down my baby and went out to cut some wood for the fire, just as I used to do, hoping that my work would mollify his passion. Before I came back into the tent, I expected that he would have killed my children in a mad fit. I had no other choice but to cast my cares upon God who had up until now sustained and cared for my children and me.

During this argument, the older Indian woman, my owner's mother-in-law, left the tent, but my owner's wife and his daughter stayed in the tent. When I brought the wood into the tent, I asked the daughter if her father had killed any of my children. She gave me a sign that he had not harmed them, and her face indicated that she herself was pleased that he had not killed my children.

It seems that the Lord, in whom I had trusted, had indeed inter-vened, and my owner did not further vent his passions on my children and me. Thus God mercifully delivered us from the wrath of this man.

A little while later the Lord struck my master with greater sickness and violent pain. My master complained about his pain in a hideous manner. When I found out about his illness, I went to another woman and asked her if my owner's wife thought that my owner would die. She said that it was very likely he would, since he was getting worse and worse. Then I told her that he had struck my little boy for no reason at all and that he had threatened to kill us all. This Indian woman told me that my owner said that the way he treated us was the reason God had afflicted him with pain and illness. She said he had promised never to treat us that way again. Soon after this he recovered, but he was never again so temperamental. He never again struck my children or me with the intention of harming us. I believed that the Lord performed this marvelous miracle.

Several weeks later, my owner moved us again to another camp. We had made several journeys before this one, but this was the longest we had ever made. We traveled for two days, mostly over the ice. The first day the ice was bare, but on the second day snow made our travels difficult and weary. I was carrying my baby in my arms, so I was more nervous and kept losing my balance and falling. I hurt myself often in these falls. On the night we reached our camp, my owner made me go after water and bring it back to the camp. But I had been sitting on the cold ground and I could not stand up to walk, and I did not know where to go to find the water. But since I had to go to bring the water back, I started crawling on my hands and knees. A young Indian woman saw me and compassionately took the kettle from me and brought back the water for me. I was immensely grateful for her compassion, especially since she had helped me out of the kindness of her heart.

I now realized why we were taking this journey. My owner was tired of taking care of us, and he was willing to make as much money as he could by ransoming us. We traveled further toward the French. The Indians held a great dance, and many other Indians from different tribes came to our camp and joined in the dance. While the Indians were dancing, I retreated to a corner of the tent in order to get out of their way. But every time they passed me as they were dancing they would bow my head toward the ground and frequently kick with as much strength as they could. Some were barefooted and others wore moccasins. The dance went on for quite a long time, and they celebrated noisily the entire time.

It was not many days before my owner returned from his meetings with the French. He was so upset when he came back that he could not bear to have me near him. The Indians made a little shelter for my children and me. They dug a hole in the deep snow and covered it with some tree limbs. This little hovel became our home for a few days, and the cold weather and hard frost made this shelter very wearisome for my children and me.

My owner eventually took me with him to the French in order to find someone who would buy me. When we came into the French settlement, my owner asked 800 livres for me. The French offered him 600 livres instead, and my owner flew into a great rage. He told them that he would build a huge fire and burn my baby and me in view of the city if he could not have his demands for 800 livres. The Frenchman told my owner to go ahead and build the fire, saying he would help my owner if he thought he could get more than 600 livres. The Frenchman spoke very roughly to my owner, often calling him a fool. At the same time, though, he spoke very kindly to me and encouraged me to be cheerful because I would be redeemed and not have to go back with the Indians.

The next day I was redeemed for 600 livres. The Frenchman asked my owner why he had asked so much for the baby's ransom when the baby would surely die after she had eaten well. My owner said that the baby would not die, for she had already lived for twenty-six days on nothing but water. My owner believed that the baby was a devil. The Frenchman said that God had preserved the baby for a longer life. My owner said that the baby was indeed a devil and that she would not die unless someone took a hatchet and killed her. This ended their brief conversation, and my baby and I were thus ransomed for the money. My little boy was also redeemed for an additional amount.

Now I had new owners, new food, and new shelter. The French were very kind to me, much beyond what I would have expected or desired. The day after I was redeemed the Catholic priests took my baby from me and baptized her according to their custom. They said that if she died before she was baptized, that she would be damned. They gave her a name that pleased them, Mary Ann Frossways. The priests told me that if my child now died she would be saved. So my French owner then told the priests that it might be best if the child now died, since she was now in a state to be saved. But the priest said that since the child was so miraculously preserved through so many hardships, she might be destined by God for some great work. Since she is still alive, the priest said, she would now glorify God more through her life than in her death. I thought this was a very sensible remark, and I hope it proves to be true.

I was with the Indians for about five months. After I had spent a month among the French, my dear husband came to me.

I cannot tell you how overjoyed I was to see him. Since two of our daughters were still being held captive, he was very concerned that we redeem them. Eventually, he recovered our younger daughter from the captors' hands with great difficulty, but he had been unable to ransom our oldest daughter. The wife of our daughter's owner intended to marry our daughter to her son when the time was right. The Indians are very civil to their captive women, not subjecting them to sexual abuse, unless they are very drunk. This civility is a commendable trait, so far as it goes.

The affections the Indians had for my daughter made them refuse all offers of ransom. After my poor husband had waited and waited, trying unsuccessfully to ransom his child, we had to journey home and leave our daughter behind among the Indians. We set out over the lake with three of our children, our servant, and many others. By God's providence we arrived home safe and well on the first day of the seventh month of 1725. I had been among the Indians and the French about twelve months and six days.

During that time God sustained me and delivered me from evil many times. I hope I will remember his providence all my life and live in obedience and love to God. With his grace and wisdom I hope I can be worthy of his love and live a life of holiness and godliness and praise the God who has called me.

My poor husband could not enjoy himself with us, though, for he deeply missed Sarah, who had been left behind. He wanted to do everything in his power to redeem her, so he set off on a second journey to ransom her. He left on his travels on the nineteenth day of the second month of 1727 and was accompanied by a relative and his wife, who also traveled to redeem some of their children. My dear husband got sick on the journey and got sicker and sicker along the way. He realized that he would not get over his sickness and told his companions that he was resigned to death in the wilderness if it was the Lord's will. He was in good spirits and sensible until the last moments, and he died in his relatives' arms somewhere between Albany and Canada. I hope that he is at last at rest with the Lord. Though my own children's loss is very great, I know his gain is much more. I pray to the Lord that he will patiently enable me to submit to his will in all things when I go through sufferings here on earth. I pray that the God and Father of all our mercies will be a father to my fatherless children and give them a blessing that makes them truly rich. I pray that as they grow older they may grow in grace and experience the joy of his salvation that comes by Jesus Christ our Lord and Savior.

Although my husband had died, my relatives left no stone unturned in the quest to ransom my daughter. They confronted the same difficulties as before. Since my daughter belonged now to this older Indian woman, the woman had plans to marry our daughter to her son. In the meantime, however, Sarah met a Frenchman who had been trading with the Indians, and the two of them were eventually married. Thus, the Indian woman's plans failed.

As best as I can recall—since I was not allowed to keep a journal during my captivity—I have given a true account of some of the remarkable trials and wonderful providence that I experienced. I never intended to talk about this experience, but I hope that my story magnifies the merciful kindness and goodness of God. I hope that the reader will be encouraged to serve God with righteousness and humility. If that happens, then I will have accomplished my purpose.

Six Weeks in the Sioux Teepees: A Narrative of Indian Captivity

Sarah Wakefield

Preface

I want to say a few words here before I tell my story. First, when I wrote my narrative I did not intend to publish it. I wrote it especially for my children. They were so young when I was captured that I wanted them to be able to read about the details of my captivity in the event that I died before I could tell them about it. I hope everyone who reads my story will remember that I am not an author, and I trust that they will not be too disappointed if they do not find lively writing here. Second, I have written a faithful account of my captivity. This is a truthful story of the horrors I suffered and the ones I was spared at the hands of friendly or Christian Indians. Third, I have not published this book to make money. I have written it to vindicate myself, for many who do not know the particular details of my captivity and release by the Indians have criticized me unduly.

I hope that readers can overlook my errors. I trust that the world will not criticize me for speaking kindly of those who saved me from death and dishonor while my own people took such a long time in rescuing me.

Six Weeks in the Sioux Teepees

My husband was appointed physician for the Upper Sioux Indians at Pajutazee, or Yellow Medicine, in June 1861.

I remember well the first day I arrived in the Indian country. One Sunday I got off the steamboat that had brought me here and exclaimed, "Is this going to be my new home?" All I saw was a single log hut and about six hundred unkempt, impoverished Indians. I wondered if I had really arrived at the place called Redwood. I soon discovered that the buildings themselves were about five hundred to seven hundred feet above the river, up on a hill. When I got to the Agency I was disappointed and frightened because the buildings were arranged on a high prairie. As far as I could see there was nothing but empty space. I really felt as if I had left civilization. When I found out on the next morning that we were going to move thirty miles farther west, I was really upset. We got ready to leave at last, and a wagon train of seven wagons and many women and children started on the journey. We were very scared as we rode along because we were carrying $160,000 in gold with us, and all along the road the Indians were complaining about the change in the administration.

Although I was nervous, I really enjoyed the ride because I had never seen a more beautiful sight than the prairie. It was covered with flowers of all kinds. The tall grass waving in the breeze reminded me of a beautiful panorama. It seemed almost too beautiful to be nature's picture.

After riding for a few miles we started to encounter little ditches, which annoyed us because they took us some time to cross. After leaving the Lower Agency, we traveled ten miles, passing through Little Crow's village. Little did I know at the time what kinds of sufferings awaited me in that place. When we got to the Redwood River, we all exclaimed, "What a romantic spot!" High hills surround the stream and huge rocks dot the valley, giving the scene a splendid grandeur. After we crossed the river, we spotted a house the government used as a schoolhouse for the Indian children. The house had three rooms, two downstairs and one upstairs. Mr. Reynolds and his wife were the teachers at the school, and the building was also the only hotel available for those going west once they had left Fort Ridgely. We rested only long enough to let our horses catch their breath after they had climbed the high hills. The Indians were very curious about us, and they all gathered around to catch a glimpse of the new "father" who had just been sent to them.

The rest of the rise over the remaining twenty miles was very unpleasant. The powerful sun beat down on us in our open wagons. We rode along well until we came to a little ditch. We would get stuck in the mud, and we all would have to get out and hitch two or three extra horses to the wagon in order to pull us out. All this was new to us, and we enjoyed it, even though the horses suffered. After we rode for a few miles, only the road looked like civilization. All around us looked like a vast lake; there were no trees or shrubs anywhere in sight. Soon, however, we came to a place the driver said was an Indian mound. I don't know whether it was an Indian mound or not, but the land was very high in this place. We saw our future home in the distance. It looked like a fort, and many flags were flying in honor of our arrival.

We came to the end of the road about three o'clock that afternoon. We then had to descend some steep hills and go across the Yellow Medicine River. The river valley was indeed a splendid sight. Here we encountered quite a large Indian village. It was a very pretty and novel sight. The river was tumbling and rushing over many rocks, and the Indians were playing their flutes, making quite pleasant music. We had to cross the river and then ascend a high hill. It seemed like we were going to some great castle, for we could see the tops of the buildings in the distance as we were going up the hill. We got to the top of the hill without any further trouble than having to walk almost all the way. I was glad when we got to our home, for I was exhausted. There were only five buildings in this place, and there was also a small brick jail where unruly Indians were kept. The Upper Agency was situated beautifully. It sat at the junction of the Minnesota and Yellow Medicine Rivers. The Minnesota was on the north side of our house and the Yellow Medicine was on the south side.

On the first night we were there we did not get much rest. We did not know too much about Indian customs except those we had learned from the Indians who had camped around our town. That night they were having councils and talking, shouting, and screaming all night long. As ignorant as we were of Indian customs, we thought that the Indians were singing songs about our death before they came to destroy us. Toward morning the noise died down and we got some sleep. We didn't sleep too long, though, because the noise of a hundred horsemen woke us up. The men prepared to fight and waited and watched, but the Indians did not attack. What was wrong? Why didn't the Indians make some sign to us? Why were they just silent, with the horrible sounds of the horses tramping? One of our men finally went down to talk to the Indians. He found out that the horses belonged to us, for we had let them out to pasture. The Indians had ridden them up from the river valley to get away from the mosquitoes. This was the first of many scares from the Indians. Often there was no need to be so frightened. Finally, though, one of these encounters was very real, as both our friends and our country now regretfully know.

There were a blacksmith, a farmer, and a doctor employed at the Agency for the benefit of the Indians. There was also a school taught by a half-Indian named Renville, who had been educated in Wisconsin. He had come back to his home, and his teacher had followed him back here and married him. They had many pupils, all Indian children. The teachers said they taught their students all kinds of manual labor. The government fed and clothed the students, but the teachers fed their own pockets more than the children's mouths. A farmer managed the hotel, and while we were there it was a nice house. We soon discovered we could be very happy, even though we were very far away from civilization.

After we had been there a few days, we learned that there was a missionary station about three miles north of us. Dr. Williamson, a good Christian and an excellent man, managed it. I learned to love his family very much; they were so kind to us all. He had lived among these Indians for twenty-seven years, and he had educated and converted many of them. Any of the students that the Williamsons had brought up were equal in learning to any white children of the same age. I have employed women educated by the missionaries who could sew or cook much better than many of the young girls of this generation can do. Many people say the Indians cannot be civilized. I think they can, but did not really think this until I lived among them. On the Sabbath I usually attended the Dakota Church, because I was very interested in their services.

Sometimes I would go to Mr. Riggs's mission, which was about two miles away from Dr. Williamson's. It was a delightful spot, and I really enjoyed my rides over to the place. The scenery around Rush Brook was magnificent. Enormous hills—almost mountains—surrounded this stream. When I was at the top of one of these hills and started coming down, I would tremble with fear for a good while. But then I forgot all danger entirely while I was looking at the beauties of the scene. Down between these hills I could see Indian men roaming in pursuit of game while their wives and children bathed in the stream. The distance from the top of the hill was so great that they all looked like little children.

I often wondered what a person from the East would think to ride through these woods unprotected, as we so often did. I often went alone with my little boy to Hazelwood. We would return long after the sun had set, and we would often pass through the Indian camp, where about five thousand Indians lived. I never knew any of these Indians to be uncharitable or unpleasant. On the contrary, they were very kind and pleasant. I was often stopped and asked to take a puff from their pipes, because Indian women smoke when they are resting as well as when they are cooking. Their pipes have long stems, about two feet long, and they sit on the ground and mix their bread and bake it, with the pipe resting on the ground, the end in their mouths.

I spent my first Independence Day in Indian country in great fear. A messenger from the Indian camp came in the morning, saying that the Indians were coming down to make mischief. They were angry because they thought they had been defrauded. We did not know what to do. There were only fifteen men there at the time, and it would be useless to try to defend ourselves against thousands. The camp commander was not there, and his temporary commander did not know quite what to do. He proposed that we go to the jail and try to fend off the Indians. In the meantime he sent his son off on horseback to the nearest fort, which was forty-five miles away, for troops. We all stayed in the jail for many hours, except for one woman. She said that the cooking had to be done, because we had invited all the mission people down for a Fourth of July party that night. If she was to die, she said she might as well die at home as anywhere. Besides, she said, if we did escape we would all come rushing back for food. During the afternoon, a friendly Indian arrived and said they had postponed the attack until the camp's commander returned. They wanted to ask him some questions before they did anything. So, we were contented and had our dance. The Indians, however, sent down quite a large party to guard our buildings; they would not allow any person to go in or out without asking that person a number of questions. We danced that night, expecting any moment that one of our Indian guards might start shooting at us. We invited some of the chiefs in after we had eaten our supper, and shared some ice cream with them. This was the first time that they had eaten it, and it seemed to calm them down. They came in and watched our dance with great pleasure. I think the Indians took a fancy to me then, for I gave them something of all we had and showed them our rooms, all decorated for this occasion. They all said the large woman was very good.

The next day our camp commander came home, and all the Indians came down, finely dressed for a council. They surrounded the warehouse, which was a large, fortified building on the west end of the Agent's house. The Agent took his interpreter, and went up to one of the upper windows and talked with them. They wanted food right away and wanted to come in and help themselves. He told them they could not come in. But these Indians started to complain that the Christian Indians were allowed in to get food every week. They grew very rude, and kept firing their guns up in the air and beating against the doors. At last the commander told them how much flour he would give them. The Indians refused his offer, saying that such a small quantity would barely give each person a taste. He did not tell them that was all we had ourselves, for our provisions had not yet arrived. Just as they were threatening him, some teams came up the hill loaded down with flour. He told the Indians that they could have all the flour the teams had, and they accepted this. Filling him with food is the only way to keep a hungry Indian quiet. If they feel like fighting before they eat, they often forget their desires after they have eaten. For they eat so ravenously that they fall asleep and during their sleep forget all about fighting.

This was the only thing of any consequence that happened during that first year of our stay.

At Yellow Medicine there were four trading houses that sold groceries and dry goods to the Indians. The traders cheated the Indians a great deal. Indians would buy on credit, promising to pay when they got their money from the government. Although the Indians did not have a way to keep track of their accounts, the traders would use their own methods of exacting payment from the Indians. As soon as their money came, the Indians would be surrounded by traders, all of them shouting at once about how much the Indians owed each one of them. One day I saw a poor fellow swallow his money, saying that the traders would not get his money because he did not owe them any. I was surprised the Indians would allow such cheating without retaliation, but it all came in God's own time, for the first death in the awful massacres of 1862 took place at these trading houses.

All the evil habits that the Indians have acquired can be attributed to the traders. The traders first brought liquor to the Indians. The traders would take the Indians' women for their wives and would have several children with them. Then after several years they would leave the Indian women. The traders first taught the Indians to swear, for in the Indian's language there are no oaths against our God or theirs.

The first year of our stay was comparatively quiet. With the exception of the Christian Indians—who were living near us as neighbors—the Indians left and went to their homes far away. At first, I found these Christian Indians to be kind and good people. The women sewed for me, and I employed them in various ways around the house. I started to love and respect them as if they were of my own people. I became so accustomed to their ways that when I was thrown into their hands as a prisoner I felt more contented and at ease than any other white person among them. I knew that not one of the Yellow Medicine Indians would watch my children or me suffer as long as they could protect me.

In the spring of 1862, the camp commander, accompanied by my husband, visited the Indians living near Big Stone Lake. They found the Indians quiet and well contented with the things that were being done for them. They seemed very pleased with their visitors.

Before he left, the commander told the Indians not to come to the camp until he called for them because he was not sure when the government's payment would arrive. He hadn't been home for long when the Indians began coming in. At first, a few of them were frightened by some murders that the Chippewas had committed among them. It wasn't long before the entire tribe arrived and camped about a mile from our camp.

They remained here many weeks, suffering from hunger, every day expecting their pay so they could return home.

After the Indians repeatedly asked for food and received little to assuage their hunger, they were told by the interpreter—who came from Fort Ridgley—to break into the warehouse and help themselves. He promised them that he would prevent the soldiers from firing upon them.

I think it was on August 4 that the Indians started their hostilities at Yellow Medicine. We were very surprised early on Monday morning to hear them singing and shouting loudly. Soon they came driving down the hill toward our camp. They were dressed finely, and we thought they were getting ready for a dance. We were soon convinced, though, that they meant to stir up trouble. They surrounded the soldiers and rushed up to the warehouse and began cutting and beating the doors to pieces, all the while singing and shouting. They were driven wild by their hunger.

I was upstairs in my house with my children. My husband's office was connected to the warehouse. I was very frightened, and I called to my daughter to fasten the gate and secure the lower part of the house against the Indians. Soon the Indians started filling up our garden. In a short time they surrounded our house and soon came to the door and knocked on it violently. I grabbed a pistol and ran downstairs and opened the door, asking them as calmly as I could what they wanted. They wanted axes, and they filled the room and followed me around until I gave them all we had. I thought they would kill me, but I knew I could fire my pistol and raise an alarm before they could get my children. However, the Indians did not become violent but left quietly. All they wanted was food; they didn't want to kill us. If all these Indians had been fed properly and otherwise treated like human beings, very many innocent lives might have spared.

After about ten minutes, they had broken into the warehouse and were carrying out flour. Soon, however, the soldiers came into the building, and the Indians had to leave the premises, but not before they made some ugly threats and cast savage glances at the soldiers. The commander went out and talked with them and asked them to give up the flour. They refused, and he was compelled to give them all they had taken and much more before they would leave. We got very little sleep that night because we all expected the Indians to attack before the morning.

At sunrise the next morning, a Christian Indian came and told us that the Indians were preparing to attack us. Since they had succeeded so well the day before they thought they would try again. We all knew that things would be different a second time because the soldiers intended to shoot at them if the Indians came again.

Several families, including my own, decided to go down to another camp about thirty miles south of ours. We stayed there for a week. While I was there, I went to Mr. Hindman's church and was very much pleased with the Indians' behavior during the services. Little did I think while I sat there that my children's and my lives would be in danger so soon, and that the person who would deliver us would be one of those men who were listening so eagerly to God's word. Surely the missionaries have done some good. Where would the white captives be now if the Christian Indians had not taken an interest in their welfare? On Monday, August 1, I returned home. My husband came to pick me up and told me that the upper Indians had left very quietly. The camp commander had given them provisions and goods and promised to call for them as soon as their money came from the government. I went home determined to prepare myself for a journey East in a few days, for we were afraid that some of the Indians might come back and cause trouble, stealing and begging all summer.

Many people who read my account will not understand about the Indian payment, so I will say a few words here about it. In June these people come to the lands that they have sold to the United States; some of them come many hundreds of miles. If the money is not ready, they expect to find food for themselves, procured at the government's expense, since that is part of the treaty. They leave as soon as they are paid, and we see very few until another year has passed. Last year they came in at the usual time, although they knew they shouldn't come until they had been sent for. Since they had all come to the camp, it was of no use to send them back again. Of course, they had to live, and the prairie is a very poor place to find any kind of wild game. These five thousand people could not remain long where they were without something to support themselves. They ate what dried meat they had brought with them, and in a few weeks they were actually starving. The children gathered and ate all kinds of green fruit until the bushes were bare.

They had several councils, and they asked for food that they did not get. Many days these poor creatures sustained themselves on a tall grass that they found in the marshes. They chewed the roots of this marsh grass and ate wild turnips. Occasionally, they would shoot a muskrat, and with what begging they could do they would get just enough so they could live. I know, though, that may of them died from starvation or from eating improper food. My heart ached to see these poor Indians, and many times I gave them food even though I knew we couldn't afford to give it up.

I remember clearly the camp commander giving them dry corn. These poor Indians were so near starvation that they ate it raw like cattle. They could not wait to cook it, and it made them so sick that they had to move their camp to a cleaner spot of land. This is one of many things I witnessed during my short stay at the camp. I often wonder how these poor Indians bore so much for so long without retaliating. People blame me for having sympathy for these Indians, but I try to think about this matter by reversing the situation. Suppose the same number of whites were living in the sight of food, purchased with their own money, and yet their children were starving? How long would the whites remain quiet? I know, of course, that they would have done differently. We must remember, however, that the Indian is a man who does not have the discrimination of a civilized person. When the Indian fights wars, it is blood for blood. They felt as if all whites were equally to blame. I do not want anyone to think that I condone the Indians in their murderous work. Many people have called me insane because of my support for the Indians. I want every person who commits murder to be hanged. But these poor Indians were dragged into this situation through fear, I'm afraid, and I think they ought to be spared.

When I was on my way home from the lower camp, the soldiers passed us as they were returning to Fort Ridgely. I was very surprised, and I said I was sorry that they were leaving so soon. I thought it was unwise for the soldiers to be leaving now, but the captain of the troops assured me there was no need for them to remain since all the Indians had left.

The Indians living near the lower camp have always been jealous of the Indians living near the upper camp. The lower Indians thought that the upper Indians were treated better than they were. The traders told the Indians that they would not get any more money, that the camp commander was going away to fight, and that they should eat grass like cattle.

The Indians always blamed the camp commander for not giving them their goods. They said many times that if he had done so they would have returned satisfied to their homes and this awful massacre would not have occurred. The commander was deceived about these Indians. He thought they were just like white men and would not dare to stage an uprising since they lived so near to the fort. He must realize his mistake now, for this was only two or three days before they started their murderous work. I don't think he willfully ignored the Indians; he simply did not know any better. He did not understand the nature of the Indians.

On Sunday, August 17, the Indians killed some people in Acton. When they returned to Little Crow's village, they asked him what they should do next. He said they should go and kill the traders and all other whites. He said they must rid the country of all whites so that the Indians could live. On Monday, they began their work of destruction at an early hour, killing the traders in their stores. When they had done this, they began their work of destruction in general. The wine and spirits the Indians found in the stores added drunken madness to the madness of despair and vengeance. Soon the Indians were wildly dancing about the dying embers of what had recently been the stores and homes of the traders. Then they passed on, killing everything they met. Their savage nature was aroused, and, bloodthirsty as wild beasts, they raced around, beating, crushing, and burning everything they had no use for.

The Indians soon spread over the country, murdering everyone in their reach. It is not generally known how the Indians abused the traders after their deaths. They broke open the safe at one store and started throwing gold at the dead bodies, filling the mouths and ears of the bodies with gold, saying, "you have stolen our money, now take all you will." But some of the Indians acted quite decently and buried many things belonging to the missionaries to save them from destruction.

Soon after dinner on Monday my husband came in and told me to get ready to go down to Fort Ridgely that afternoon instead of waiting for the stagecoach. Someone who had come to our camp on Saturday wanted to return to the fort and said he would drive us if my husband would let him take our horses and wagon. We started our journey at two o'clock that afternoon. I felt unusually sad; I remember going from room to room taking a final look. My husband got impatient and asked me what I was doing, so I made some flimsy excuse. I knew he would make fun of me if he knew how I felt. As we were leaving he told the man taking us to the fort to drive fast and to get us there early. I asked my husband why he wanted us to hurry, and he gave me some answer that satisfied me at the time. Many times while I was in captivity I recalled this conversation. I asked the man driving us if he had a pistol, and he said he had. But he didn't have a pistol, because after his death no weapons of any kind were found on him. We drove to a trading post, and one trader said that he had heard some bad news. The Indians were killing people over in the big woods and the Indians were getting very ugly. The lower Indians as well as the upper Indians were holding councils about whether or not to kill the whites or to leave for Redwood River.

I was anxious to go back to my home, but the man driving us made fun of me. He said that he didn't think that the upper Indians would make any trouble. Besides, he was in a hurry to get home, and he would send four or five hundred of the friendly Indians to fight for the whites. He told me that my husband had heard these same reports, and that was why he was sending me to the fort. This man was misguided, for all day the lower Indians had been killing people and we, not knowing it, were going into their country for safety. I rode in great fear that afternoon. I was very sad, and death seemed to be hovering near me. We didn't meet one person or living object as we rode, and I said many times to the driver that something must be wrong below us for we usually met teams on this road constantly.

Mr. Gleason, our driver, was in high spirits. I had never seen him so happy before. He was laughing and singing, he was so happy. When I chided him and told how nervous I was, he simply said that he would never take me anywhere again because of my nerves. I tried to get him to go back with me, but he said that I would live to see the time when I would thank him for taking me away. He tried everything he knew to make me feel comfortable, but it was no use. I had a strong feeling of evil, and it was a premonition of what was to happen. As we got nearer the mound that was between the upper and lower camps, we could see clearly the smoke of the burning buildings. I said to him that the Indians were destroying the buildings in the lower camp. He said that they weren't but that the smoke was coming from the sawmill or from a prairie fire. I was so scared that I tried again to persuade him to take me back. I was so excited that I could not sit still and tried to jump out of the wagon. Then he became very angry and told me how unpleasant it was for me to act that way. "Okay," I said to him, "let's go ahead. They will not kill me, but they will shoot you and take me prisoner." "What are you talking about?" he asked. "The lower Indians are just like white men; please don't get so hysterical." By this time I was crying.

Soon we saw a little house, and he said to me that I had been acting foolishly, for this house was still standing. It was near six o'clock, and Mr. Gibson said we would stop at the little house to eat dinner and then be at Fort Ridgely by eight o'clock that night. He had hardly said this when, as we were going down a little hill, I saw two Indians approaching us. I told Mr. Gleason to take out his pistol, but he said that these Indians were just some boys going out hunting. So I asked him to make the horses go faster, but he drew the horses to a halt and asked the Indians where they were going.

We were sitting in this open wagon, with Mr. Gleason sitting directly in front of me, and my little boy by my side and my baby in my lap. As the Indians passed the wagon, I turned my head to look at them because I was suspicious. Just then one of them shot at Mr. Gleason. The bullet hit him in the shoulder and he fell back into my lap, crushing my baby against me. He did not say anything and immediately the savage fired again, hitting him in the stomach as he lay across my lap. Mr. Gleason now fell backwards out of the wagon as he turned toward the Indians. What a sight this was for a mother! My thoughts ran away with me, for I thought they would shoot me next.

When Mr. Gleason fell out of the wagon, the horses began to gallop away. The Indian who had not fired the gun ran after us and caught the horses. As he came up to the wagon, he asked me if I was the doctor's wife, and I told him I was. He then said, "Don't talk much; that man (and he pointed to the Indian who had shot Mr. Gleason) is a bad man. He has had too much whiskey." As soon as he had quieted the horses, he came to the wagon and shook hands with us. A small ray of hope entered my heart. My hope was soon dispelled, for when we turned around where Mr. Gleason was writhing in his death throes, I saw the other Indian loading his gun. I expected every minute to be launched into eternity. When we rode up I begged this Indian to spare me for my children's sake, and I promised to sew, wash, cook, cut wood or anything rather than to die and leave my children. He did not speak, though; he only scowled hideously at me. Chaska—the good Indian—urged me by his looks to be quiet. Just then Mr. Gleason spoke when Hapa, the savage Indian, shot once again, killing Mr. Gleason instantly.

Even now as I write, this scene appears very clearly before me, and I can hardly hold my pen. I never can feel worse than I did that night. I imagined my death many times during my stay on the prairie. But this event seems so clear to me now that I cannot keep from trembling; even so, I have to write about it. In a moment after Mr. Gleason breathed his last, Hapa stood on the wagon and aimed the gun at my head. He would have killed me if it had not been for Chaska, who leaped toward him and knocked the gun out of his hands. I begged Hapa to spare me, pleading for my life with my hands outstretched. He knocked them down. I thought that my doom was sealed, and if it had not been for Chaska, my bones would be bleaching on that prairie and my children would be with Little Crow. Three or four times did this demon try to destroy me, when Chaska would pull him away by the arm. I could hear Chaska tell Hapa of some little act of kindness my husband or I had shown them in years gone by. All Hapa would say was, "She must die; all whites are bad, better be dead." Can anyone imagine my feelings, exposed as I was to being shot every moment and not knowing what my fate would be if I were spared?

I think these two Indians argued about what to do with me for nearly an hour. Chaska tried everything he could think of to persuade Hapa to leave me alone and let me live. So many thoughts ran through my head then. Death was nothing to me if my children were dead as well. But it was agony for me to think that I had to die and leave them to whatever fate might have in store for them. I could see them left to starve to death or partly murdered, lying in agony and calling for their dead mother. Father in heaven, I pray that you will impress my thoughts at this moment upon an ungenerous world that blames me for trying to save the man who rescued me from death when it was so near. After a long time, Hapa agreed that I should be allowed to live. He was satisfied that I was not the camp commander's wife. Chaska knew that I was not, for he had been at my house many times. He often told me that if Hapa could have captured the camp commander's wife he would have cut her to pieces just because of her husband.

Chaska and Hapa climbed into the wagon, and we left poor Mr. Gleason on that prairie alone with his God. Unfortunate man! If he had only listened to my pleas, he might still be alive today, and I would have been spared six weeks of painful captivity. I rode along in great agony because I didn't know where they were taking me or what my fate might be eventually. I turned around to look one last time at Mr. Gleason. Just at sunset I bid him goodbye forever, but Chaska told me not to look at the dead man anymore. Chaska told me that Hapa was very angry and that he would kill me if I turned around anymore.

Hapa sat facing me all the way, and kept his gun pointed at my breast. He kept saying, "I will kill those children; they will be trouble when we go to Red River." But Chaska said, "No; I am going to take care of them. You must kill me before you can kill any of them." Chaska was a farmer Indian who had dressed in white man's clothes for several years, had been to school, and could speak some English and read and spell a little.

Hapa was a wild "Rice Creek Indian," a horrid, bloodthirsty wretch. The good work of the missionaries can be seen clearly in the differences between these two Indians. The two men were vastly different, although they belonged to one band and one family. The teaching that Chaska had received made all the difference, though. Although he was not a Christian, he knew there was a God, and he had learned right from wrong.

After riding for a few miles, we reached the Indian camp, which consisted of about two hundred people. When they found out who I was, their laments touched me very deeply. They turned out to be old friends of mine. Six years earlier I had lived in the town of Shakopee. In the winter this same band that I now found myself among was camped around the town. Not a day passed that some of the Indians were not at my house. I felt sorry for them and gave them food. When the battle between the Chippewas and the Sioux occurred near Shakopee, many Sioux were wounded, and my husband took care of them. They often said that he saved many of their lives. Now that I was with them they said they would protect me and mine. When they helped me out of the wagon, many of the older women cried like children. They spread down rugs on the ground for me and gave me a pillow, telling me to lie down and rest. They fixed my supper and tried in every possible way to make me comfortable. That was impossible, though. They promised me life, but I dared not get my hopes up and felt as if death were staring me in the face.

I hadn't been in the camp very long when a half-Indian came up to me and said he felt very sorry for me. He told me that I would probably be spared for a few days but then that I would eventually be killed, because they had sworn to kill everyone who had white blood in their veins. He did me a great wrong, for he knew better than to make my fears worse. He was a great rogue.

After the older women had given the children supper, Chaska told me to come with him to a house where there was another white woman. He told me that the Indians were not going to sleep in teepees that night, and he thought that my children would get cold sleeping out on the prairie. I was afraid to go with him, and I asked the half-Indian what I should do. He told me to go with Chaska: "Chaska is a good man; you must trust him, and you will be treated well." He then gave me some very good advice. He told me as long as I was with them that I should try to be happy and not to mistrust them. I should make the Indians think that I had confidence in them, and they would soon learn to love and respect me. That would be the only way of making my life longer. So I followed his advice and never gave them an angry look. If they ever told me their plans or their adventures, I would laugh and say, "That is good; I wish I were a man; I would help you." When they were preparing for a march or for battle, I was as busy as anyone else in the camp. I prepared the meat for the warriors. I helped paint blankets, braided ribbons to decorate the horses, and tried every way I could to be useful, hoping that

I could then gain their friendship. I knew I could reconcile myself to them in that way; if I had acted differently, I would have been treated differently.

I accompanied Chaska and left my trunk of clothes in the wagon. I was carrying my baby in my arms and leading my boy by his hand. We walked for about a mile. I was suspicious, but I kept up with Chaska. I talked to him about the heavy dew that was falling so that he would not think I was frightened. He stopped at a hut, for I guess he wanted to show off his prisoner. While I was there the Indians brought in Mr. Gleason's clothes and his watch, which was still running. I looked at it and saw that it was eight o'clock, the exact time he said we would be at Fort Ridgely.

The Indians were entertaining themselves by laughing at his empty pockets. He had no pistol; he had deceived me. Since it was unsafe to go anywhere without a gun in those days, I often wonder why Mr. Gleason did such an unwise thing. There was a white woman in this hut, but I did not get to know her or find out her name. She was a German, and her greatest trouble seemed to be the loss of her feather beds. She had seen her husband killed, but that was very little compared to her other losses. All through the night, this woman would moan and sob and begin to wail: "All my five feather beds are gone. I picked the feathers myself in Old Germany, and now they will not give me one to sleep on." She said that after the Indians killed her husband, father, sister, and brother, they were about to kill her. But then she said to them: "Don't! I will give you my house, everything I have, and I have much money." So they spared her. She said that the Indians forgot her money, they were in such a rush to get away with her and her goods. After they crossed the river, she went back alone to get the money, which she had hidden away. I think it's very strange that they did not murder her, for they had all her possessions anyway. She was an unhealthy woman, and she had a two-week-old baby. She declared that the Indians had not abused her, and she said they were very kind to her. She only mourned the loss of her feather beds.

The Indians asked me to take off my whalebone hoops, and I did so. I would have cut off my right hand if I thought I could have saved my life by doing so.

We stayed here only a short time before we went to another house where I met another woman. They had a good fire and plenty of candles, and made me as good a bed as could be expected. I was told to lie down and go to sleep because we were leaving for Red River in the morning. Sleep was far away from me on that night and on many others, though. After Chaska had made us comfortable, he left us in charge of some older women and boys. He told me to go to his mother's hut in the morning and to ask her for an Indian dress, for he said I would be safer wearing such a dress. The German woman and I managed to make it through the night, but she did not speak English very well. Still, she was a white woman.

No one can imagine what it's like in an Indian camp when the young warriors come home victorious. There is such confusion it is as if all hell has broken loose. Hour after hour we listened to every footstep, expecting to die at any moment. They were firing guns in every direction; women were mourning over their dead, and the magic healers were working over the sick and wounded. All of this increased the confusion in the camp.

At last morning came. As the sun rose, the Indians started leaving our camp. They were going to attack Fort Ridgely. Since it was quiet, I went to see Chaska's mother, and I was soon transformed from a white woman to an Indian woman. Even under such circumstances it was very humiliating to put on such clothes. The day, Tuesday the nineteenth, was extremely hot, and I began to suffer. My hat and all the other clothes I possessed were gone. I thought I would suffer from heat stroke, for we were constantly moving. The Indian women would get frightened and pack up, and we would move on. We repeated this several times during the day. Once they heard that the Upper Indians were coming, and the women rubbed dirt into my skin to make me look more like an Indian. Surely I did not look like a white woman. I did have the pleasure of looking at myself, though, since the Indians had placed a large mirror belonging to Mrs. Reynolds against a fence. They were having a fine time admiring themselves in the mirror, too.

I sat down by the roadside while we were waiting for news from the fort. I tried to disguise my children. I rubbed dirt all over my little boy, but his white hair would likely give him away. I tore the skirt off my baby's dress and took off her shoes and socks, but did not rub dirt into her skin. She is naturally dark-skinned, and the Indian women said she looked like an Indian baby after I made her look wilder by tearing her clothes.

During the morning, an old woman named Lightfoot came and sat down by me. She said they were going to kill me in a few days, but that they were going to keep my children. When the children were grown, she said, the Indians would get a great price for them. I became frantic when she told me this. I thought about this all night, and I decided I would kill my children rather than leave them with these savages. I ran to an Indian woman and asked her for a knife. I grabbed my little girl, and I would have cut her throat in a minute when another Indian woman told me that they were not really going to kill me. I wish every mother could imagine what I was suffering when you think of me trying to cut my own child's throat. If my children were only dead and out of trouble, I could die willingly. I supposed my husband was dead, so I was living only for my children.

About four o'clock that afternoon, Chaska's mother came into her hut. She told me that a man was coming to kill me. She lifted Nellie, my baby, onto her back and told me and my boy to hurry. She stopped at the hut where I had stayed the previous night and told an old man her story. He told us to flee to the woods. She gave me a bag of crackers and a cup, and we ran to a ravine. It was very steep, and the banks were like the roof of a house. When we got to the bottom she hid me in the tall grass and underbrush. She told me to sit still and left me there, saying that she would come back to get me in the morning.

I have endured many trials, but I never suffered as I did that night. God willed it that a furious storm broke out as soon as the sun had set. But I did not fear the storm, for I felt that God had sent it for my benefit; still, we suffered from the storm's effects. The rain and mud washed down on us from the sides of the hill, drenching us completely in a few minutes. I had only one blanket and tried to keep my children warm with it. I had a small bottle of brandy in my bag, and as my children awoke that night I gave them some in their drink. It kept them from catching cold. My heart beats with fear when I remember that night.

Surely God gave me strength or I would have died from my fear. By nature I am a very cowardly woman. Every leaf that fell during the night was a footstep, and every bough that cracked I imagined was a gunshot. My nerves were so weak that my heart-beats sounded like someone running, and I would frequently hold my breath to listen. Muskrats looked like wolves as they crawled around me in the darkness. I thought they were wolves that were going to eat me. I sat all night, my foot in a running brook. I did not dare move, for I was afraid that I might make some noise that would lead them to discover me. I could hear the Indians racing around, firing guns, singing, hooting, and screaming.

Many people who read this will think I was foolish to give in to my fears. But you cannot tell what you would do or how you would feel. Many times now I think I was foolish; still, I have no doubt that I would feel the same again under these circumstances. My children would often wake up, and I would tell them to be quiet because the Indians were nearby. The little darlings would lie close beside me, trembling with fear. I don't know how I was able to live through that night, but I know God was with me. I passed the time in prayer. I thought of my husband and my friends lying murdered in their blood. I begged God to spare them if they were still alive. I know he heard me, for we now know how narrowly they escaped.

Can anyone imagine how I suffered? No, they cannot. Even now I do not realize my agony. Just for a moment, imagine a woman at any time lying in the woods alone all night. We would all pity the person in that situation. Think of me again. I was down in those deep, dark woods; I did not know where I was or how long I might be there. I felt that one day my bones would be found. My mind was full of tortured thoughts that awful night when devils incarnate were rushing all around, looking for whom they might eat, and when the elements of heaven were all at work. My little boy would wake up at times and say: "Momma, take me home and put me into my own little bed. Why are you just sitting here? O, momma, do go home. My father would not want his boy to stay outside all night long." I would then whisper to him about our troubles, and he would say: "I forgot about the Indians; I will be still; I have been asleep and dreaming."

After a flash of lightning, I would pray for the next bolt to strike me or else save me to meet my husband. I never knew how to pray before, but I had no one to call on but God. I knew he could save me and I begged and pleaded with him all night. I will never forget his goodness, and I can never stop praying to the One who brought me out of such dangers.

Finally the morning came. I was sorry to see the light because I thought that we would be discovered and our fate sealed. Hour after hour passed, and the Indian woman did not come. It was now quiet where it had been so noisy all night. We could hear nothing but the birds singing and the brook running.

I now began to think that she had forgotten me and left the area, and that my children and I would be left to die in this ravine. I knew I could not climb these banks by myself, and our bag of crackers would not last very long. I was now afraid that we were going to starve. Our situation was truly horrible. We were completely covered with mud, and now that the sun was shining the mosquitoes were all around us. My children's faces were running with blood from their bites, but my darlings were very quiet, for they were so afraid that they did not notice the stings.

After waiting for several hours, I saw the Indian woman coming. I was overjoyed to see her. We laughed and cried, and I think I must have kissed her. I felt as if our deliverer had finally come. She carried Nellie on her back. I tried to get up, but I could not. I had been sitting too long in one position, and the water had chilled my blood so that my circulation had stopped. The Indian woman rubbed my legs and feet, and she told me that the men who were going to kill me had left. I should try to walk to her hut, and she would give me some dry clothes and some coffee. She said that the Indians had moved across the Redwood River and this was why it seemed so quiet in the morning.

We left when I was able to walk. She carried both children up the bank and then helped me up, for I was not strong enough to walk up the bank by myself. I had not eaten at all in the past two days. The exposure and fright, along with the fact that I was nursing a twenty-month-old child, had weakened me considerably. When we arrived at one hut, the woman gave me a cup of coffee and some painkilling medicine; this revived me greatly. We walked about three miles, stopping at every hut for some coffee or tea. She would make me sit down and warm myself, for I was shivering with fear and illness.

At last we came to the Redwood River, and we started crossing it. In some places the water was up to my shoulder. The old woman continued to carry my baby, and I carried my little boy in the places where he could not walk. But this child was as brave as a man, and he ran along through the woods that morning with scarcely a word, the bushes tearing his feet until the blood was running from them. Sometimes he would yell out, but I would shake my head and tell him that the Indians would hear him. Then he would remain quiet. I knew the little fellow was suffering very greatly, because even I could not bear my own suffering without an occasional groan.

We did not travel along paths or roads, but through the tallest and thickest brush. We did not stop to part the bushes but tore through them like wild beasts driven by fear. Of course we cut ourselves badly. I am completely covered with scars that I will take with me to my grave.

After crossing the river, we arrived safely at the Indian camp. They had not yet built any huts, but they were getting dinner, each family by its wagon.

I felt comparatively happy when I came to where my home was supposed to be. I had endured so much in the past night that even the women seemed like friends. And they did turn out to be good, true friends. Poor women! I pity so many of them. They are driven from their good homes, and their families are broken up and divided. We should feel as sorry for them as we do for the white women.

When I had rested a while, they gave me my dinner, some dry clothes, and water with which to wash my children, and they prepared a bed for me to sleep in.

I discovered that Chaska was still away from the camp. He and his mother were living with Hapa and his wife, who was Chaska's half-sister. Her name was Winona, and I was afraid of her, for she was just like her husband, who had murdered poor Mr. Gleason. She tried in every way to make me unhappy when Chaska was not there, but she was very good when he was around. She took my trunk of clothes and made them her own. She would not give us anything from this trunk to wear. So the older Indian woman who had accompanied me would go around and beg when my children needed clothes. She would not give me a pin to fasten my slip, and I had to sew it together. She took my embroidered underwear, dressed in them, and then laughed at me because I was so dirty and unkempt. One day her son was playing in the dirt with a shirt collar that I valued highly. I asked him to give it to me, and he did so. But she took it from me, tore it to pieces, and threw it in my face. One day I told Chaska I needed my slip because mine was so dirty. Winona gave me some cloth to make one. A sudden rain shower soaked my new slip, and the colors faded. Chaska saw that this was no good, and he became angry. He caught Winona by her hair, slapped her in the face, and abused her shamefully. At last I persuaded him to stop this, but he said she was a bad woman. She took my earrings from my ears, put tin ones in their place, and began to wear mine. She cut up my silk dresses and made coats for her boys to wear while they were tumbling around in the dirt. She would destroy all small objects, like my miniatures, and she would laugh when she saw how sad I felt. I would like to be her judge if she is ever brought within my reach.

After lying quiet for about an hour, many women surrounded me, talking about some evil that threatened me. The older Indian woman said that there was a bad man who wanted to kill me, and that I had better go again to the woods. I told her I could not because I was completely exhausted. So I would simply stay here and face death. I stood up and looked out to see what all the excitement was about. I saw women being led into a hut by an Indian wearing a white band on his head. I would hear a shriek and see women's clothing laid out and what we all thought were bodies being loaded into a wagon and being driven off. A German came to where I was hiding under the wagon and said we were all to be killed in a short time. He said the women were very excited and wanted him to hide in the woods, which he thought was useless. The old woman soon came back and said: "You must not talk; I will cover you and your boy with buffalo robes." Taking my baby on her back again, the woman kept marching back and forth, as if she were guarding me.

I made up my mind to die. I knew if Chaska were near that he would save me. I talked with my son in a whisper. I told him to remember his and his sister's names and asked him to stay with her always and take care of her. If his father or uncle were still alive he might be able to find them one day.

Several times I peeked out from the robes and asked the woman if there were any news. She was crying and said, "Chaska is dead, and you will die soon. That man is a very bad man." I cannot begin to describe how I felt. I know I prayed. I begged God to save me from savages. Sometimes I cried, then I would get calm; at least once I began to sing. I thought I would try to go to my death cheerfully. At last I felt perfectly happy, and I believe if I had died then, I would have died a Christian. I had said goodbye to the world. I thought my husband was dead and all I had to live for was my children. I hoped that they might die with me. I told my little boy, James, who was five, that he would soon die and go to heaven. He said, "O Mamma, I am glad, aren't you? For my father is there, and I will take him this piece of bread." The poor child was not old enough to know how he was to reach that happy land.

I asked Winona how we were to be killed and she said we would be stabbed. I dreaded to die that way, for I was afraid we might suffer for some time. While I sat there thinking of my sad fate and how my friends would feel when they heard of my death, I though I heard a neigh from our horse that Chaska had ridden away on. Soon I heard her mate, who was tied near, respond, and I felt a sudden thrill, as if my preserver had come. In a moment Winona raised the robes and said to come out, for Chaska had come and everything was all right. I did not need to be invited twice. I went out, and sure enough, there he stood. He shook hands and said, "Don't be afraid; he will not dare to hurt you while I am near. If he comes near, I will shoot him." I was so happy! Once again he had saved my life. Hadn't God raised up a protector for me from among those who did not know him? Don't I have many reasons to bless his name, and to thank the man and his family for all their goodness toward me and mine? My little children would now be motherless if he had not taken care of me.

I spent the rest of the day quietly. That night we had a violent thunderstorm that blew down our hut. We had to spend the rest of the night huddled under the wagon on the wet grass, while the rain poured down on us. That was quite a scene. When we got up from the wet ground, we could see fires in every direction because the storm had blown over nearly all the huts. It looked like a picture I had seen where witches were holding their revels. The scene looked like this because there were old women sitting around the fires singing and smoking their pipes. They seldom sleep anyway. They usually sit smoking their pipes until the day begins and then they go to bed after they have said a prayer to the sun. I often sat in the night and watched them as they smoked, talked, and cooked, until I thought that their magic spells were working on me. They often took the form of devils in the midnight hour, singing and moaning over their fires in their half-awake state. Nights like this did not help my already heightened imagination. At times I was nearly frantic. In addition to these witches' revels guns were being fired continually. I really thought that every gunshot sent some poor creature into eternity, and I expected that my turn would come any minute.

On Thursday, August 21, the Indians were up very early, preparing to attack the fort. Chaska was going, but he was afraid to leave us where we were. He was afraid that Hapa might return and kill us. He told me that I better go to his grandfather's with him. Chaska's grandfather lived in a brick house about a mile from where we were. The wagon was ready soon, and my children and I and the older Indian woman began our journey. Before we left, Winona painted my cheeks and a part of my hair. She braided my hair with several colored ribbons and dressed me in fancy colored clothes and shoes. She and others painted my children in a similar way. Then she gave me a blanket and told me to start traveling. Who would have known I was a white woman? Even I forgot who I was sometimes, especially when I looked around and saw the way I was living. If I had not had my children with me, I would not have stayed and allowed myself to be dressed and painted in such a manner. I would have tried to escape, and if I died while trying, then it would have been fine with me. As it was, I did not dare try, for I knew they would have discovered me and certainly would have killed me. I know that after the first few days is the best time to try to escape, and I often urged young girls to try to escape. I know I could have run away if my children had been large enough to walk. But they were too large for me to carry, and they could not walk very far. We were free to go wherever we wanted. We could go down to the river, pick plums, or go from hut to hut to visit. I often walked down to the Minnesota River to get water, and I would stand there and make plans to escape. The water was so low that we could cross the river. Once someone crossed the river, I knew that she could have hidden herself and returned to the settlements without being discovered.

That morning the prairie was full of Indians. They were all in high spirits, and they were confident that they could overrun Fort Ridgely. They were either overly dressed or else they were not dressed at all. Their horses were covered with ribbons, bells, or feathers that jingled or tinkled as we rode along. The Indians sang their war songs lustily. The sight of these great and powerful men on their decorated horses going off to war was a grand but savage sight. Many of the men were entirely naked except for their breechcloth, their bodies painted and highly ornamented. When we traveled over this same road a week earlier, I would not have imagined that I would be a part of such a war party on its way to kill my family and friends.

We arrived at Chaska's grandfather's house at sunrise. The morning was very cool, so the fire in the stove over which they were cooking breakfast was very comfortable. There were several huts around his house. I discovered that I was with some of my best friends in the Shakopee Band. An older Indian woman that the whites called "Mother Friend" was there, and I was glad to see her. Chaska left soon after I had eaten my breakfast, saying that he would stop for us the next night. I passed this day in great fear. We could hear the cannon at the fort and see the smoke from the burning buildings. From where we were camped we could see much of the battle. We could see the Indians fire their guns, run back to the woods and reload, and then attack the fort again. I expected every minute for one of them to return and to destroy us in their rage. Nearly all of them were drunk, and just about every day one of them would look at us and tell us that they were going to cut off our heads. We heard many stories about the progress of the battle. Sometimes we would hear that the Indians had all been killed and that the whites were coming. At other times such confusion ensued that we fled to the ravines and hid ourselves in the bushes. The Indian women were very afraid, and they needlessly frightened me many times. My children feasted on this day, for one family had enough nuts, candy, and maple sugar to open a candy store.

I shall never forget Mother Friend's kindness on that day. She would not let me stay in the old man's house, but made me spend the day with her. She made my little boy new moccasins, brought water and washed my dress, carried my baby around on her back, and did everything she could to lighten my sufferings. When the old grandmother called me in to dinner, Mother Friend would not let me go. She told the grandmother, "No, she is my child. She has given me cooked food in her hut at Shakopee; now she must stay and eat bread with me." Her daughters tried every way to amuse me, and they would tell me that their father would take me down the river in a boat when he came home. Although their father was kind, he never offered to take me down the river as they promised.

At sunset a messenger arrived, saying the Indians were going to stay all night. He told us that a chief was coming to kill us white women, for there were three of us there in the camp. They told me to run into the woods again. Eagle Head, Chaska's grandfather, said he would go with me. He was nearly eighty years old. Mother Friend told me to leave James because he was asleep, and she would take care of him. The old man took his gun, and I took my baby on my back. We ran into the woods, where we roamed all night until daylight. We stopped only long enough for me to nurse my baby. When we heard the Indians shouting we would run farther into the woods. The old man could not keep up with me. He would say, "Stop, I am tired; I will die." I would wait for him. As dawn approached, everything grew quiet. We came out of the woods onto the bottomlands of the Minnesota River. He said he would go back to the camp after he hid me. He would not dare take me back until he could find out how things were. He pulled out the center of a haystack and hid me in the middle. He then covered me up with the hay. I thought he would be gone just a short time. But hour after hour passed, and it was soon noon. I thought I would suffocate or die of thirst. My baby was very hungry. I had not eaten anything, so I was very weak and had very little with which to nurse her. I sat for hours that day nursing her—for she was pacified when I nursed her—and I thought I would faint from the constant drain on me. I could hear the water running, but I did not dare come out of hiding. I had seen Indians very near us twice that day. My baby was fretting, and I nearly choked her when I heard Indians coming. I clasped my hands around her throat until she was black in the face, for I knew her cries would lead to our discovery and death. I'm sure my poor baby thought her mother was very unkind, for she would look so pitiful when I would put my hands around her throat. But this action saved our lives.

I sat this way until sunset. I thought night would never come. I was even more miserable because of my son. I knew he would be crying himself sick because he had never spent a night away from me in his life. Oh, how I blamed myself for leaving him, but I had expected to return in a few hours when I left him. Where was my child? I was afraid that he would scream and cry and that some hostile Indian would kill him. Just after sunset I heard a voice and some footsteps nearby. I did not dare speak, though. In a moment Chaska's grandfather poked his head into the haystack and told me to come out. I was overjoyed to see him. He told me not to talk loud, for many of the Indians were hostile. I asked for some food and drink, but he told me I would have to wait until I got to the hut. It was a while before I could stand up, for I had sat in one position, with my feet drawn up under me, for eighteen hours. As soon as I could stand, we started to walk back to the camp, and I found out we had to walk for several miles. I didn't think I could live to walk so far, but strength was given to me.

I asked Chaska's grandfather if he knew anything about my son, but he didn't. Every gloomy thought I had experienced during the day rose up again before me. I was almost sure he would be dead when we returned to camp. But I knew Mother Friend would save my child if at all possible.

As we walked along we passed through a muddy piece of ground. I dipped up the filthy water in my hands and drank some and gave some to my baby. The water was refreshing, but I think a dog would ordinarily refuse to drink such water. However, my mouth was parched with thirst. Many times during the day I had reached my hand into the middle of the haystack to find some moist hay. I would draw this hay through my lips to try to moisten my awfully dry mouth and throat.

I think we walked about four miles. I asked everyone we met about my son, but no one knew anything. At last I arrived at the hut. My son was not there, but Winona came in and said he was very near. In a moment he came in, and I was overjoyed. My heart was bursting with joy! He ran into my arms and cried, as if his little heart would break. "O, momma, I thought you were dead, and I was left alone with the Indians. I have cried until I am sick. O, dear momma, are you really back? Do kiss me, and keep your arms around me. I thought you and Nellie had gone to heaven and left your boy all alone." He told me that he had slept through the night and that Mother Friend had told him I would be back soon. After he ate his breakfast, Winona carried him on her back to her hut. He said he had cried so much that a half-Indian had taken him to see an ox killed. But my son said that he thought that I might have met the same fate as the ox, and this made him cry even harder.

I could not get him out of my arms that night. He clung to me in his sleep, and trembled with fear if I tried to lay him down. I sat and held him all night. I watched the stars through the opening in our hut and wondered if his father could see us in our captivity.

I soon found out that they told the Indian who came to kill us that we were at the large encampment. Of course, we were already well hidden when they told the Indian this. The Indian searched for us in the woods, but he decided to wait until the next morning to kill us because he was lazy and tired. Apparently he didn't want to kill us but to rape me. What do you think about the way that I was treated by the other Indians? Don't I owe these friendly Indians a debt for my life and honor? You can imagine what my life would have been like that night if they had not saved me. I can never express my gratitude to those who were so friendly to me when I was in such danger. Let other people blame if they want to. God, who knows all things, will judge me, and I will wait and bear all the world's reproaches, knowing that with God all will be well.

We woke up early on the next day because we were supposed to leave for Yellow Medicine. The Indians decided to wait until Tuesday to leave, though. Soon after dinner, an Indian called Chaska out. When Chaska returned, he said, "I wish I could kill all the Indians." I asked him why. He told me that an Indian in the next hut was drunk and had threatened to shoot all the white women in the camp. Chaska told his mother to close the door to the hut and to keep watch. Just then I heard a gunshot and a woman shrieking, "I am shot!" Chaska's mother said that the Indian had shot the white woman in her legs as she sat outside the hut.

Chaska was very alarmed. He sat down and told me to sit behind him, taking my children in my lap. If the Indian came in, he had to shoot through Chaska before he reached me. We sat this way for a long time, until Chaska's mother told us the Indian had passed our hut. We then fled out of the back door into the woods, his mother carrying Nellie on her back again. She found a good place for us, covered us with tree boughs, and left in a hurry, without saying when she might be back. I sat for a while. When I heard running water, I thought I would try to follow it, for it would surely lead me to the Minnesota River. I put Nellie on my back, and we followed the brook for a good distance. We then came to a place where a large tree had fallen across the brook, impeding our progress. I decided to stay here since it was a very good hiding place. We sat in the water until sunset when I heard the old woman calling, "White woman, where are you?" She had been to the place she had left us and was very frightened to find that we were not there. She followed our tracks along the stream, and appeared delighted to see us again. I was certainly delighted to see her honest face. As she took my baby on her back, arranged my blanket around my shoulders, and placed my hair around my face to conceal it, I could not help giving her a good kiss. I learned to look upon her as I would upon a mother, and I hope one day to be able to do something for her.

She said that a large number of Indians had just come in from the fort, bringing many mules. This seemed like a good opportunity for me to go back home, since the Indians were very excited about the things they had stolen from the fort. We were near our hut when she saw the Indian we had been running from. She hurried me into her hut and covered me up with robes, telling me to remain as quiet and flat as I could. Then the other Indian women threw their other robes on top of me. The old woman left, but not before she told the other Indian women to feed the children. Soon some Indians came into the hut and asked to whom the children belonged. The women said that the children's father and mother were dead. I thought my little boy might speak up and tell them who he was, for he could speak Dakota very well. But he did not. All during our captivity he demonstrated the good sense and reason of a grown man. In a few moments the Indian who had threatened me came in and asked if a white woman was in the hut. The women said no. I can assure you that my heart beat fast with fear and trembling, for I did not know these women at all. I didn't know whether or not they would betray me. While I lay there, an Indian boy came and sat down on the robes. Fortunately he was there only a short time or else I would have suffocated. I couldn't breathe deeply because I was afraid he would notice the motion of my body. Soon Winona came in and told me to hurry back. We went home and had a good supper. I was glad to lie down and rest, for my feet were so sore I could hardly walk. My left foot was covered entirely by sores, poisoned by weeds, and constantly irritated by running through the prairie grass.

I always felt safe when I was in Chaska's hut. He always warned me not to go out of the hut when he was away, for he could not guarantee I would be safe from drunken Indians. He really didn't need to warn me, though, for I really had no desire to run around. Traveling was enough movement for me. Many of the white prisoners roamed around during the day and often asked me to walk around with them. I always refused to join them. I was happiest when I could sit with the old woman and have her wash my feet and take care of my sores. I felt as if this were my home, and I stayed there all the time I was in captivity. For that reason I was treated better than any other female.

I thought I was better off staying there and taking care of my children than roaming around the camp and gossiping, always in danger of being shot by the Indian soldiers. The Indian camp was the worst place for gossip I have ever seen. Several of the half-Indians spoke good English, and they reported to the Indians every word that we white women said. Thus many things were exaggerated and misunderstood because they went through many translations. I was always careful to speak well of the Indians, supporting them in their actions. I knew whatever I said would be repeated to them. My sole purpose was to gain their friendship so I could save my life. I hope that God will pardon me for any deceit I used in this way.

I slept very well on Saturday night until about midnight when Hapa came home. As usual he was drunk. He woke all of us up by his drunken actions, but I didn't think he would harm me while everybody was in the hut. I pretended I was asleep. But soon he asked where the white woman was. I dared not speak or move. I thought he would kill me for sure, for a drunken Indian does not know what he is doing. I whispered to the old woman, asking her what I should do. She told me to lie still, for Chaska would not let him hurt me. Hapa soon got up, drew his knife, and walked over to me saying, "You must be my wife or die." I asked Chaska to come to my aid, for I was certain Hapa would kill me. Chaska told me to lie still, for he would take care of me. He asked Hapa what he wanted, and Hapa told Chaska, "She must be my wife or die." Chaska said, "You are a bad man; there is your wife, my sister. I have no wife, and I don't talk bad to white women." I told Chaska to let him kill me, but to kill my children first. He turned to Hapa, who had his knife drawn, and said, "Go lie down. I will take her for my wife, for I don't have one." Hapa said, "That is right; you take her, and I will not kill her." Chaska said that he would marry me as soon as he knew that my husband was dead. But Hapa insisted that Chaska must make me his wife right away.

The old woman told me not to be afraid, for Chaska was a good man and would not injure me. Then Chaska said to me, "You must let me lie down beside you or he will kill you, he is so drunk. I am a good man, and my wife is in the spirit world and can see me. I will not harm you." Chaska lay down between his mother and me, and Hapa returned to his bed contented. He was soon in a deep, drunken sleep. When Chaska thought Hapa was asleep, he quietly crawled back to his own place and left me as he found me. My father could not have acted more respectfully or honorably. If there was an honest and upright man, Chaska was one. God will certainly reward him in heaven for his acts of kindness toward me. This was not the only time he saved me in such a manner. Very few Indians or even white men would have treated me like he did. I was his captive, so why didn't he abuse me? He knew that it was a sin. He knew I was married, and he always intended to give me back to my husband.

Many believed that I was his wife, and I did not dare tell them otherwise. I encouraged everybody to believe this, for I was afraid that Hapa would discover that we had deceived him. I didn't think about what people outside the Indian camp thought, for I had my doubts about ever getting away. I guess I thought that if I was ever so fortunate to get back that I could explain everything. I never once thought that people would think of me as a liar, as many now call me. After all I have experienced, it is sad to receive so many reproaches from those I thought would feel sorry for me.

Our hut blew down again on Sunday morning, and we had to sit under the wagon and wait for the old woman to go to the woods and cook our breakfast. The winds were so high that the women could not cook on the prairie. A number of white women visited me on this day. They said they heard I was married, and asked me if that was my husband. I said that I supposed my husband was dead and changed the conversation, for there were many around who could understand everything we were talking about. These women walked away and said that I had acknowledged the rumor. This is the truth, and I am very sorry that women would do such a thing toward one of their own sex.

On Sunday afternoon, I think they must have decided to kill the prisoners, for Chaska came home soon after the Indian soldiers came in off the warpath. He whispered something to his mother, and she turned to me, saying, "Bad, bad." She got me some stockings and a new pair of moccasins, washed my feet and put them on. Then she started off for the woods, telling me to let James go with her. James started to go, when I looked at Chaska, whose face told me that he blamed me. I ran after James and took him back to the hut with me. The old woman was very angry. I don't know what was wrong. But I have always thought that she was going to take him away so he wouldn't see me murdered. She talked with Chaska and told me to go inside the hut. Soon he left on horseback. That night as I laid my children down to sleep, I had strange and conflicting thoughts. I was sure my death was near, for the Indians always clean the feet of a person who is about to die.

I was in bed when Chaska came in with two Indians I had never seen before. He said that I had to take my children and go with him. I asked him where we were going and what was wrong. He said that sometime he would tell me. I woke up my children, and we all left. I didn't know what was in store for me, but I trusted him and went along with him. Chaska carried James, and I carried Nellie, and the two Indians walked along side us as guards. It was dark and rainy, and I was at these men's mercy, walking toward an unknown destination. Since Chaska had always been honest with me, I found no reason to distrust him now.

We walked a long way and left our camp far behind us. I started to get a bit suspicious, but Chaska kept telling me to keep quiet. We arrived at a small camp, and he took me to his aunt's hut. He told her that I should stay there. They whispered together for a while, and she looked at me very sadly. Chaska left, telling me that he would return in the morning. I never found out why he took me there; I imagine there was some threat of danger. I was certainly well cared for by these people. Would white people treat me as well? About this time I heard that my husband was dead. The Indians who were returning from Yellow Medicine told me he had been shot and his head had been cut off, and that the rest of the people there had been massacred in some horrible manner. You can imagine what thoughts I began to have then. I felt that life was not worth living. I wanted to die right then, for

I had always hoped he would eventually rescue me. Now all I had were my children. Would they be spared longer? I could not know, but God spared us all. I thank him for his goodness.

The Indians were as respectful toward me as any white man would be toward a lady. It upsets me terribly when I hear people insult the Indians. I know some who are as manly, honest, and noble as whites. I stayed at Chaska's aunt's hut all the next day. Around nighttime Chaska and his mother came, and she told me I had to go. The Indians were coming and we would be leaving for Yellow Medicine the next day.

As we were going home, I saw an Indian who cried out, "There is the doctor's wife." I smiled, but the old woman told me to hurry on, for he was a Sisseton Indian and he would kill me. I was not afraid, as I knew the Sissetons would take care of me; I longed to go to Yellow Medicine. I knew the Sisseton chiefs would not allow Little Crow to kill me. He was constantly threatening us, especially me. He was determined to destroy me, for I was the only one of the Yellow Medicine people that he had captured. He often said that I should die because they had escaped. This caused me more trouble than any other woman suffered there.

One day, while I was still at Redwood, a half-Indian told me there had been a council and that all the whites would be killed very soon. I sent for Shakopee, the chief of the tribe that I was with, and asked him if I was to be killed. I told him I would help kill the other prisoners if he would spare me. I also promised never to leave his band, and that I would help sew and chop wood and be like an Indian woman. I was so afraid that I really didn't know what I was saying, and I didn't care. "If I can only live just a little longer, and get away," I thought, "my husband, if he is still alive, will not care what promises I made, if his wife and children are saved."

The promises I made to kill my own people were awful, but I was nearly crazy; I expected our soldiers to come any time and wanted to live to see them. Many unthinking captives, hearing my remarks, have told them to the world since my release. This has caused people to believe that I meant all I said. However, I was afraid to die, and I was horrified by death at the hands of the Indians. One day the old woman seemed very worried about something, and I didn't know what it was. Chaska was away from home. Soon I heard gunshots, and I imagined they were shooting the white women. I imagined this next scene, so you can imagine what state my mind was in.

I sat under the wagon on this day. Near us was another wagon that I sat and watched all day. I imagined it was full of dead bodies, and that buffalo robes were covering the bodies. I could not see the bodies, but their hair was hanging out from beneath the robes. Sometime during the day, Winona came in with a piece of skin. I thought she was going to place it around my throat after she cut my throat. But this was just a piece of an ox's tendon that she sewed with, and the hair I thought was human was from the buffalo robes. I passed a frightful day. I suffered as much as if this all had been real. I often wonder whether or not I was entirely crazy.

We got little rest the night before we left for Yellow Medicine. The women were packing and the men were preparing for battle, for they had heard that the soldiers were coming. We started our journey at the first light. My little boy had diarrhea, so I had to take off his pants, and he traveled that day wearing nothing but a shirt and a breechcloth.

I had no moccasins to wear that day, for Indian women travel barefoot, and I had to do the same. Although they were in a great hurry, they still took time to paint my cheeks and to braid my hair. When we started on our journey, there were Indians in every direction, as far as the eye could see. The old woman grew very excited and told me to hurry because the Sissetons were coming and would kill me. I had to carry my baby on my back that day. I had never heard such noise and confusion. My little boy was crying that he could not walk so fast, and Nellie often slipped down my back nearly to my feet. Nellie would cry and the old woman would worry because I could not keep my baby on my back. If I stopped, she would reprimand me and tell me to keep moving. When we got to the river, there were teams of horses stuck in the mud and there was much confusion as everyone tried to free them. In addition, the Indian soldiers were galloping in every direction, shooting their guns, not caring whom they trampled. I was afraid we would be crushed to death.

Fortunately the river is not very deep in the summer. If it had been, many of us poor females would have drowned. I had my baby on my back and was holding my boy by the hand, and I had a hard time trying to keep us from being swept away by the current. Sometimes the water was up to my shoulders, and I would have to take my boy in my arms, which was quite a burden for someone like me not used to such labors. As I was trying to get through, an Indian rode up to me and asked me where I was going. I told him I was going to Yellow Medicine. He said, "You are the doctor's wife?" I replied that I was an Indian woman, for the old woman had just whispered to me that this was a Sisseton Indian. He laughed and told me he knew me, "You must not lie. You are not an Indian woman, for your eyes are too light." When we had crossed the river, this Indian stopped near the ruins of a house and called me over to him. He whispered, "I am Paul; don't you know me? You must come with me to my hut."

I knew Paul very well at Yellow Medicine. He was a farmer Indian, but he was dressed in his Indian finery, so I did not recognize him. He wanted me to ride, but I did not dare ride a mule bare-back when I had never ridden a horse with a saddle. My little boy knew Paul well, and he was anxious to go with him. I said to my child, "You will cry when the night comes, because I shall walk and not get to Yellow Medicine for two more days." My son replied, "No, no, momma, I will not cry. It will kill me to walk so far; please let me try to go with Paul." I asked Chaska, who had just walked up, if I should try to go with Paul. He talked with Paul for a few minutes and said I could go with Paul if I wanted to. Chaska warned me that Paul wanted me for his wife and had been trying for several days to find a white woman. He said that Paul had also told him that my husband was alive. They had all escaped from the camp the morning after I had left. This was glorious news for a wife who had already mourned her husband. I laughed and cried and acted like a wild woman. I could have danced for joy, my body and mind felt so light. Now I felt like I had to live and save my children. From that moment on, I had a new purpose in life.

I told James he could go with Paul. He told me as he rode away that he wished I could go with him, and he seemed a little sorry that I had let him go with Paul. Even now I can see those little legs hanging down against the black ones of the Indian, and his white face looking so pitiful as he rode away. I regretted many times that day that I let him ride away. Sometimes I would think that it might not be Paul after all, that I had been deceived, and that I would never see James again. I thought he might have a heat stroke riding on that hot day without a hat to cover his little head. Everywhere we went I expected to see his body. I suffered so much in my mind that I did not realize how much my body was suffering. The more I thought, the less hope I had of seeing him again. Then I realized that God could shield James from danger whether he was with me or not. I said a prayer for him, and I felt calmer and more settled, knowing he was in God's care.

I walked along barefoot, traveling through the tall, dry prairie grass in great distress. In some places the grass was five feet tall. The grass cut my feet and legs as it switched around them. We also stepped on many prairie snakes. I had to keep up with the Indian women, and they run as fast as horses.

At noon we stopped for dinner. We had crackers, maple sugar, and cold water. When Chaska saw my feet, he told me that I had to ride, for all the skin was torn off one foot and both feet were bleeding. His mother washed my feet and wrapped them up in clean roots. They gave me a seat on the wagon, and I drove the horses the rest of the day. I don't know how I could look at poor Mr. Gleason's body as we passed it. He had been stripped of his all his clothes except his shirt and underwear, and the Indians had crushed his head with a stone. I was now traveling again toward what had once been my happy home, which was now destroyed and desolate. The one with whom I had last traveled that road was now lying there dead. I could not help rejoicing that my bones were not lying there as well. How I wished I had power to punish Hapa right then and there, although Hapa never even looked at the remains of his victim. Perhaps his conscience bothered him for what he had done.

We did not travel very far after dinner, because we heard white soldiers were pursuing us. All of a sudden there was disorder everywhere. Everybody ran to a little thicket, for everyone knows that this is the Indian's battleground. Here they prepared to fight. Guns were fired and reloaded, powder flasks were filled, and every Indian got ready for action that night. We camped two miles away from water, and I thought I would die from thirst. But Chaska soon came in with a large bag of plums, which refreshed me a great deal. You can imagine what I was thinking as I sat under the trees with these people. I didn't know where my husband was. I didn't know where my boy had gone, because I still didn't know whether or not I could trust Paul. Sometimes I thought they were going to take me to Yellow Medicine and murder me in sight of my home. I felt certain that Chaska's family would protect me as long as they could, but every day we heard reports of Indians murdering their prisoners.

The Indians had a soldiers' lodge where they conducted all their business. They always go there when they return from battle and make their report. As soon as they can, they send out a man who tells everyone the news, whatever it is. Every few days, as the Indians would come in we would hear the cry, "White women to be killed now very soon; they eat too much. We are going away and they cannot travel; they had better die at once." Of course, this agitated our minds a great deal. I don't know how I lived, but there was One above who was giving me strength, or otherwise I would have not been able to survive.

The Indians did not put up many huts the night we camped there. Nearly all of them slept under their wagons to guard their horses or goods. They were constantly afraid of some evil. They did not enjoy their plunder very much or for very long. We started our journey to Yellow Medicine very early. When we got there our houses looked just the same as when we left them. When the people fled, they left everything. The Indians soon broke into the houses and robbed them of all kinds of food and other things they could use in their own huts, but they left the large furniture in the houses. When we got to the top of the hill, I had to get out and walk. Everything looked so different from the time I had left it.

Very soon we had to climb the hill on the opposite side of the river. It was around noon, and the sun was so hot that I was nearly crazy with a headache and anxiety. I had lost the old woman, and Winona would not wait for me. I had to run to keep up with her, for she said that if I stopped the Indian soldiers would kill me. After we reached the top of the hill we walked for another two miles before we stopped. We set up our camp, but there was no shade around. I thought I would die before I was able to get any rest or water. While I was sitting on the grass with my sick child, I heard Good Thunder's wife say that she had water. I begged her to give me a drop for my baby, who was try-ing to nurse from me. She told me to get some water myself. She had some boughs she had put up to screen herself, and I sat down in their shade. But she soon drove me away. I was very surprised, for they were Christian Indians. Afterwards, I found out that Hapa and Good Thunder were good friends, and the latter was mean to me because Hapa was. They eventually occupied my hut and divided my clothing between them. Mrs. Good Thunder cut up seven of my dresses in one day, laughing because they were so large. I cannot begin to describe my sufferings on that prairie, without shade or drink. I had not yet seen or heard anything from my son. If I could have had him with me, I could have borne all my other troubles patiently.

About this time some trouble arose between the old woman and Winona. Winona accused the old woman of stealing some shot. They had a terrible argument, and Winona threw a tin kettle at the old woman, who left, saying that she would not stay with Winona any longer. When Chaska came in I told him what had happened, and he said he would leave. Hapa was forever threat-ening my children and me because we ate so much. He told me to go to his grandfather's hut. His mother was there, and Chaska would soon come and join us. I went to their piece of ground, for they were not going to put up their tents that night. I had to sleep under a wagon for another night. All the sleep I really got was during the daytime, for I was too nervous to sleep at night.

After we arrived at Yellow Medicine the next morning, the Indian soldiers decided that our camp should be in a circle. The old woman got scared and hid me again for several hours. I could not find anyone who knew where Paul was. I did not know his Indian name, and they did not know him by the name of Paul. Chaska said that if Paul did not bring my son that night, he would go in the morning to Hazelwood, for Paul used to live there. My feet were not in good shape either. One foot was infected, and the old woman told me that I shouldn't walk any more for several days. Soon afterward she brought me out of my hiding place and carried me to the camp. Everything was very quiet. She took me to her sister's hut. She made me a good breakfast of coffee, fried meat, potatoes, and fried bread. But I could not eat because I was thinking so much about my son. While I was drinking my coffee, a woman came to see me. I had known Mrs. Decamp at Redwood and at Shakopee, but I had not seen her since the days before my captivity. She was not feeling very good and complained to me about the way she was being treated. She said she had no decent place to sleep or anything fit for a pig to eat. She begged if she could have my food for herself and her children. I felt very sorry for her, for many nights she said that she and her children were driven out of the hut while the medicine men tried to heal a wounded man who was with them.

That afternoon, just as I had bandaged my feet nicely and Chaska had gone after my son, someone said the Indians were getting drunk. At first I wasn't alarmed until Chaska drove excitedly up to the hut. He said a drunken man had just killed a white woman and that I must hide somewhere. An old woman I had known at Yellow Medicine said she would take me up to the friendly camp of Yellow Medicine Indians. She took Nellie on her back and we ran for some cornfields, stooping down so no one could see us. We ran through the fields and at last arrived at the hut, exhausted. Unless a person has run for her life, she does not know how it feels to be so relieved after reaching a safe place when she has worried about being captured and killed any moment. When I got to the hut, I got on my knees and thanked God once more that he had saved me from death.

That night I was very happy. Someone told me she had seen James that day and that he was well and happy. The man who owned the hut prepared some medicine for my feet that eased the pain very much. The hut's owner was Chaska's cousin, and he was a very good man. He was a farmer at Yellow Medicine and one of my nearest neighbors.

The morning after I arrived at Chaska's cousin's hut, Chaska brought my son. At first I didn't recognize him because he was dressed so differently than the last time I had seen him. As I ran toward him, he was busy showing some toy to the Indian children around him. He didn't seem too happy to see me. I asked him if he was glad to see his mother, and he said, "Oh, yes, but I had such a nice time at Paul's, I want to go back again." He acted older, even though he would not be five for a couple of months. That night I was very happy, for I had both my children in my arms. I thought I would never be unhappy again if I could only keep them with me. I knew my husband was alive, and that I was out of Hapa's reach. I sang to my children that night. We ran around the prairie and picked flowers, and my spirits were as light as air. Many people say I was happy with the Indians because I did not grieve over my situation as many people did. Why should I grieve all the time? Would that do me any good? I would have felt worse if I had done so. I tried to make myself as happy as I could while I was with my Indian friends. Because of this, they learned to respect me more every day. I felt the change from civilized life to savage life as much as anyone would, but it was not helpful to keep making comparisons between these ways of life. I tried to be as content as I could under the circumstances.

After I was in this camp for two days, some Indians said I should go back to Chaska's, for Paul had decided that he was going to make me his wife. I would be safer with Chaska than at this camp. An older Indian woman sent for Chaska, but when he did not come by nightfall, she carried Nellie on her back and we left. We met Chaska along the way, and we rode with him in his wagon back to his aunt's. James was upset because it was raining and he was wearing a new Indian costume that Paul's wife had made for him. He was afraid that the rain would ruin it. I went to Chaska's aunt's, and Chaska told me to stay there until his mother could put up her tent. Before this war, Chaska had lived in a house, was a good farmer, and worked hard. When he was forced to leave his house, he went with his sister and her husband, His wife had been dead a few months and he was still wearing mourning clothes for her. I stayed with his aunt, helping his mother make our hut. We sat out in the hot sun sewing, the white cloth drawing more heat toward us. I was afraid I would hurt my eyes in this bright sunlight. But the only change in my body has been in my color; I don't think I will ever recover from this sunburn.

On this day I saw Mrs. Decamp again. She was very unhappy, and begged me to ask her Indian owners to give her a dress because I could speak Dakota. She and her children were very dirty. She came in one morning and said she was starving, so I gave her the food I had left over from my breakfast. She sat a long time and talked about our situation. Several times she said she would be thankful if she could be as comfortable as I was. I told her that she was not being smart in her relationship with the Indians. She cried all the time and this made them angry with her. They gave her the best they had and she should try to be patient with them. If she kept on complaining, her life would be in danger because such behavior only made the Indians angrier with her. One day she heard all the Indians had been killed in a battle. She was very happy, like all of us. I tried to restrain my feelings, but she did not. She cried out, "Oh, that is so good. I wish all of them were dead; I would like to cut their throats." She grabbed a knife and flourished it as she said these things. That was not very smart, for several Indians understood every word she said. One of them stood near her and said in Dakota, "You will die for talking that way." Not long after this, she went up to a half-Indian's place about a mile away. Soon she disappeared entirely, and we all imagined that she had been secretly murdered, for the Indians disliked her very much. Chaska often told me not to bring her into our tent, for the Indians would then learn to dislike me as well. But she escaped and got to Fort Ridgely not long after her husband's death. She had told me that my husband was really dead because she had heard an Indian say he had seen the body. Her words paralyzed me, for I kept hoping he was alive. Once I could speak, I told her that if my husband really were dead then I might as well spend the rest of my days in this camp as in any other place. "My husband was everything to me," I said, "and I don't have any more desire to live; life will be a burden to me." This lady was determined to look always for the worst in every situation, and no one could bring her any comfort. My feeling is that God sends our trials, and I must bear them as well as I can, trusting him to deliver us from all evils.

I went to Chaska's cousin's again, but I don't remember how long I was there this time. I do remember that I was with them after the battle of Birch Coolie, for we got up the next morning and moved farther up in the country. I looked at my home with sadness, for it was engulfed in flames on the morning we left. I didn't have any high hopes of seeing that place ever again, for the Indians said they were going to the Red River now without stopping again. I thought I would certainly die before we got there. Chaska had always said that the soldiers would come soon and rescue me before the river began to freeze. He promised me that if they did not come, he would take me down the river in his canoe. I told him I had better wait for the soldiers, for if the Indians discovered us they would kill us. I tried to be courageous, but I was very sad as my children and I drove across the prairie that day.

I had driven many horses, but not one as wild as this. He was an Indian pony and perhaps had some mule in him, for he would often do the opposite of what I directed. I was both amused and frustrated, and I often think how funny a picture we must have made. It was quite a task to keep everything in order that day.

Considering everything, we traveled along pretty well. When we came to a creek, the pony plunged forward without regard for the wagon he was pulling. He was so thirsty he just had to get a drink. We all got stuck in the mud. Finally, with the help of an Indian girl, we were able to get the horse and the wagon out of the mud. I was completely covered with mud from my struggles.

We got to the other side of the creek, and everything except my blanket was safe. We rode the rest of the way quietly, but my son would ask every now and then, "Momma, why don't you turn around and drive to Shakopee?" I told him that the Indians would not let us. He said, "Momma, why do you suppose God made Indians? I wish they were all dead, don't you, momma?"

We camped about three miles west of Hazelwood, but it was a long time before the Indians could decide on the best place to set up camp. On this day, they gave us bread and molasses; the children thought this was a great treat. While we were sitting under the wagon and eating our treat, another woman captive came to me. I knew this woman was a prisoner, but I had not seen her since I had been in captivity. She looked very nice in her Indian dress, but she did not mention my looks at all. She told me she would not have known me if she had met me on the prairie, for I had changed so much: On the night I was taken prisoner I was so frightened that my hair had turned as white as an old woman's.

Chaska's cousin told me she would like me to stay, but that I would be safer with him. So they asked him to come and get me. He didn't want me to leave his cousin's, for if I went with him I would have to walk. He had only one horse now because he and Hapa had parted ways. But all I could think of was my life, and I preferred to go with him even if I had to walk because I didn't want to stay here expecting every moment to be killed. Chaska and another one of his cousins came to get us. One of them took Nellie and the other took James on their horses, and I followed along by their side.

I think I suffered more mental anguish at Yellow Medicine than anywhere else because it brought back so many pleasant memories. It reminded me so clearly of my home and of the days when my husband and my children and I had been united as a family. What was our fate now? Would we ever be together again?

I got back to Chaska's tent, and it seemed so good to get back here, for everything was so clean, new, and sweet. About this time, my baby got quite sick, and I thought she would die. Someone told me that I could find medicine in Dr. Williamson's house, which had not yet been destroyed. I asked Chaska to take me there, because it was several miles away and I didn't dare go by myself. One day Chaska took James, his cousin, and me to this house that I had often visited. What a change! Their once happy home was all destroyed. It looked as if an earthquake had hit the house, for everything was broken and thrown together. How my heart ached as I passed through the rooms where I had often seen the friendly faces of my friends.

Why have these Indians lived so quietly for so long, and never, until this late day, done any wrong toward the whites? I could think of only one cause, and I may be right about this or I may be wrong about it. I believe that our own people, not the Indians, were to blame. Hadn't these Indians been cheated unmercifully? Their money had been delayed, and their "father" had left them without money, food, or clothing and had gone off to war. I often said to the Indians that if they had let innocent people alone and simply robbed us all, they would never have been blamed. However, the only way they knew how to achieve justice for wrongdoing was to kill people.

I sat down on the door stoop and cried. I couldn't help thinking about how dramatically my situation had changed in the two weeks since my capture. My son then said, "Don't cry, momma. You know we shall get away soon." So for his sake I dried my tears and put on a cheerful face.

While I was at this camp, I had great difficulty bringing water from the creek to the camp. The ravine was almost perpendicular, so I had to pull myself up by grabbing twigs. Sometimes I would slip and fall back down the bank and be drenched by the water. One day when I went to get the water, I thought I would wash my feet since they were dirty. Since I could not reach the creek with my feet, I thought I would put some water in the pail and put my feet into it to wash them. Then I would wash out the pail before I got water to take back to the hut. When I returned to the

hut, there was a great commotion. Chaska brought in an interpreter, who said that I had committed a great sin by putting my
feet in the pail. All vessels that belong to a tent are sacred, and no
women are allowed to put their feet in them or to step over them.
I told him I could scrub the pail, but he said it would not do, for
they would never use it again. And they never touched the pail
again. They turned the pail upside down and left it on the prairie
when we left the camp.

The Indians had many interesting superstitions. Their war
spears and medicine bags are sacred, and women are never
allowed to touch them. During the day, these things are tied to a
pole in front of the tent, and at night they are brought inside and
tied high above the head of the chief man in the tent. One morning
I noticed that these things were about to fall. As I went toward
them to fasten them tighter, an old woman said, "Stop, white
woman, stop, I will call some man." She appeared very frightened,
and brought over a boy very quickly. When the men go to battle,
they always take their spears with them, thinking that a few
painted sticks will help them in their efforts.

I offended many an Indian god by stepping over axes, pipes,
people's feet, or some such silly thing. They never wash their
hands in any dish; they fill their mouths and then spit it out on
their hands. I could not do this, so they found me a wash dish
from some half-Indians.

I don't remember when during the month we started our journey for Red Iron's village, but I can tell you that I suffered a great
deal on that day. I had to walk all the way. I could not ride my
horse because the Indians were using it to pull a wagon. They put
James on her back, and I carried Nellie on my back. We walked for
sixteen miles without resting even for a drink of water. They
seemed to feel bad because they could not give me a ride, but it

was no use to complain. Everybody had a load, so I just plodded on. Sometimes when Nellie fell asleep the old woman would put her on the wagon. She was fine until a jolt from a bump woke her up, and then I would have to walk as fast as the wagon to comfort her and keep her quiet. The sun and dust on the prairie did not add to my looks. I would hear the Indians say, "White woman has a dirty face," but I had no idea how I looked until I went to the river to arrange my dress. I experienced more pain than ever before in my life during the last few miles we traveled that day. Someone could easily have tracked me by following the blood that ran from my feet and legs. I was glad when we stopped, and I told Chaska that I thought I would die if I had to walk any further. He said he was sorry, and he asked me to stay at his cousin's so I could ride. I told him that I would rather stay with him and his family than go back to his cousin's and risk being killed.

We stayed at Red Iron's village a little while. One morning two men left with letters to Fort Ridgely. Soon afterward the Indian soldiers left, crossed the river, and everyone believed that they had gone to kill these two men. A great alarm arose in the village, for the Indians said that if the soldiers killed these two that they would return and kill the rest of the half-Indians and prisoners. I could not speak for a while when I heard this; my teeth chattered and I shivered with fear. I then remembered that Chaska told me many times that if I were in danger to tell the Indians I was his wife, and I would be saved. So I said to an Indian that I was Chaska's wife and asked him if they would kill me. He said they would not, but I didn't believe him. I went back and told Chaska, and he told me I had done very wrong, for there was no truth in my story. I had not thought about how my story would sound, but I would have called myself the evil spirit's wife if I thought I could have saved my life by doing it. I suppose many

Indians really thought I was his wife, but in the midst of all this excitement I didn't even think about denying it.

One day, a half-Indian woman and Mrs. Decamp came in. They told me that Little Crow was going to destroy all the whites but would spare all those who had Indian blood in them. I said I was safe because I was part Indian. I knew Mrs. Decamp didn't believe me, for she had known me in Shakopee for many years. I said that I was about an eighth-breed, for my grandfather had married an Indian woman many years ago in the west, took her east, and I was one of her descendants. I then asked her if she remembered how very dark my mother was, and that convinced her. I was sure that this half-Indian woman would tell everyone, and I would be spared. I know it was wrong to tell such lies, but I felt as though my God knew my thoughts and that he would pardon me for doing what I did. To this day, Mrs. Decamp believes I am part Indian, for I never had a chance to tell her otherwise.

While we were at Red Iron's village, the camp was quiet. The soldiers would go off on scouting parties, but most of the Indians sat around playing cards or shooting at ducks. The women were busy drying corn and potatoes and laying in a stock for the winter. I helped out willingly with all these activities, for I thought I might be able to save my children from starvation on these plains where we were bound. I had given up all hope of being rescued.

I did not have many idle moments. I made short dresses for the women, made bread, fried meat and potatoes, brought water, and went to the river to wash my baby's clothes, for her diarrhea was growing worse daily.

The Indians were all very kind to me; they brought me books and papers to read, and I would make them shirts to return the favors. Many times when I had been climbing the steep banks of the river—all out of breath and carrying water—some Indian would take the pails out of my hands and carry them for me. Now for a white man this would not be considered a great thing, but for an Indian it is a great thing, for they never carry wood or water. I remember many little acts like that. There are indeed many good and kind-hearted Indians. One day I was down by the river waiting to fill my pails when I saw an Indian approaching. I was standing near a tree resting my head against it. He came very near to me and spoke in English, "Mrs. Wakefield, this makes me feel very bad." Then I recognized him. He was a Christian Indian who had been at my house. His wife had worked for me all one winter, and he knew I was suffering very much carrying water. He got off his horse, shook hands, and burst out crying. I sat down on the ground and cried for almost an hour with this man. Even though he was an Indian he gave me such good advice that most people would have been astonished. He told me to put my trust in God. He told me never to forget that God had the power to save. If I could feel that God's eye were on me and that his arms were around me, everything would be well. He said he would do all he could for me, and that he had often prayed for me. This was certainly evidence of God's love. This man stood firm in God's truth even though he was surrounded by savage and heathen Indians who continued to encourage him to forsake the white man's God and return to worshiping sticks and stones.

After we left Red Iron's village, we rested very little. The Indians knew the soldiers had left the fort, and they expected the soldiers would come soon. I ran for the woods many times with the Indian women, thinking that the soldiers were very near and that they were going to shoot their cannons at the camp.

Every night now the old women kept their doors open so they could watch over their horses. We were getting near to

Sisseton territory, and their chief Standing Buffalo had threatened to take all our horses and cattle.

If Chaska and his mother had not been so kind to me, I would have certainly suffered greatly from the cold. They lent me their blankets, and they made sure there was always a fire so we could keep warm. Where could you find white people who would go without cover to keep others warm? This was a great kindness.

The Indians made fun of the slow progress of the white soldiers. They said that the white people must not care much about their wives and children or they would have come faster to their rescue.

Many nights the Indians would announce that the soldiers were coming and that they should get ready for battle. Sometimes they would say that the white women were to be killed in the morning. When morning came, they would tell us a different story. This was dreadful way to live. Little Crow had a plan. When the soldiers came he was going to send the white women out in Indian dresses, so the white men would kill the ones they had come to rescue. I was not afraid of such a plan. Chaska was very nervous when Standing Buffalo came to our camp. The lower Indians were very afraid of the Sissetons, and they thought Standing Buffalo would kill the white women. But he came and shook hands with some of us, and he said that if the Indians brought us to his country he would take us back to our friends.

When we found out that the soldiers were very close to Yellow Medicine, the Indians prepared to go out to fight them. I was very uneasy then, for Chaska and his cousin were going out to join the battle, and I would be without his protection. When he and the others left, I had a terrible day. We heard all kinds of reports about the friendly Indian camp that Little Crow had threatened before leaving. Later that night Chaska returned and told us what a bad man Little Crow was. He told us he would not go again unless someone forced him to do so, and he stayed with us for two days.

One morning a messenger came, saying that every man that could carry a gun should come down immediately or be shot. I urged Chaska not to go, but he said that Little Crow would accuse me of preventing Chaska's going and kill us both. He urged me to stay with his mother and not to talk to any half-Indians or other white women or to go to the friendly camp. After Chaska had been away for a while, a half-Indian told me that Little Crow intended to destroy the friendly camp as soon as he returned.

I stayed with his mother as I had promised to do. If Little Crow had been victorious, all would have been killed. But God ordered otherwise and they were saved.

Chaska was away two days and one night. When he came back, I asked him how the battle had gone. He said they had killed 150 white men and lost only two Indians. I felt as if all hope were now gone, and couldn't help saying that I believed the Lord was on their side. But the great moaning and crying of the Indian women that night told a different story. They grieved all night for their losses. Chaska told me to lie down so my shadow would not show on the tent sides; he was afraid they would shoot through the cloth and kill me.

They held a council that night and decided to give us up. I was told that a letter would be sent to the soldiers the next morning, asking them to come and get us. They had many plans. They started packing in the morning and getting ready to move again. I asked if they were going to give us up to the army. They told me that five half-Indians would take us down to the white soldiers. I told them I would not go, for I believed that Little Crow's men would kill us all. Soon the camp began to break up, and the old woman gave me some roasted potatoes to eat since we were going to the plains where we could get no more potatoes. I became upset and Chaska asked what was wrong. I said that I did not want to go with the Indians. He said, "You do not wish to go with the half-Indians; what will you do? The Indians will be leaving very soon." I told him I thought the Indians were going to wait for the soldiers and try to make peace. He said they were afraid to stay, for they were sure they would all be killed. In the meantime they asked me to write an account of my treatment by Chaska and the other Indians. I told them it was very foolish for me to write such a note, for I could just as easily tell people my story. I started to suspect some evil here. I was afraid they would murder us, hide our bodies, and carry our notes to the fort. However, I wrote the note, but I was determined that I would not go over the prairie with the protection of just five men.

Soon after I had written my note, they told me to hurry and change my clothes to those of a white woman. Since the soldiers were coming it would not be right for them to see me dressed like an Indian. I dressed in a great hurry. At last we were ready, and we left our hut and my Indian friends, who had given me a home and protected me for six weeks. The old woman shook hands with me and kissed me. She said, "You are going back to where you will have good, warm houses and plenty to eat, and we will starve on the plains this winter. Oh, that 'bad man' who has caused so much trouble," referring to Little Crow. They cried over James and begged me to leave him with them. He was a great favorite with the Indians all the time I was with them. Chaska, his cousin, and my children and I started out for the Indian soldiers' camp. A large American flag was flying above us as we sat down on the grass, and we sat there waiting for our captors to decide whether we would be staying or going.

Everyone seemed anxious for us to go, but none of us, except for a few half-Indians, wanted to go. At last they said they would carry us down to the camp, and I resisted mightily. I declared I would not go with them, and so one of the Indians said I could stay with his wife, who was a white woman, until he came back. We stayed on this hill until Little Crow's camp had gone, and then we went over to the friendly camp. Chaska and his mother said goodbye to me and left.

The half-Indians came back from the white soldiers' camp in the afternoon. All night long we expected the white soldiers to arrive, so we got no sleep. Every person was on guard. We dug trenches around out tents, for we expected to be attacked before morning by Little Crow. His brother had stayed around to spy on us, and we were sure he would tell Little Crow that the soldiers had not appeared.

We had a very anxious night. The morning dawned, but we could still see no soldiers, and we wondered what was the matter. Some Indians came in, saying that they had returned because their band was not large enough. Chaska, who had returned earlier, became frightened. He told me that I should go off with some half-Indians and take his mother with me. I persuaded him to stay, promising to protect him. He said he felt as if the soldiers would kill all the Indians, but we told Chaska that if the commander had promised to shake hands with all the Indians who stayed behind to give up their prisoners, the commander would keep his promise. At last he decided to stay, saying. "If I am killed, I will blame you for it." Now I will always feel that I am responsible for that man's murder, and I will chide myself for urging him to stay.

We looked for the commander all the next day, but he did not come. We watched all night as well, but there were no signs of him. We wondered where he could be, since he was just twenty-five miles away. Finally, we concluded that he was afraid. The Indians started to get worried and said that Little Crow would soon kill them if the white soldiers did not come. We blamed the commander for making us worry so much, for we expected to be killed any moment. The commander and his army certainly took their time getting to us. But God watched over us and held back Little Crow's band. I give him all the honor and glory, and I cannot even thank the commander, for he did not deserve it.

The second night of our stay the Indians held a religious ceremony. The women were excluded from it. They were trying to determine whether or not the soldiers would hurt them.

Every Indian was on guard that night because we had heard that Little Crow was getting closer to fight us. There were no more councils or dances; all was quiet except for the medicine men, who were doing their performances over the sick. The Indians believe that people are possessed with evil spirits when they are sick. These medicine men stand over the sick people and rattle gourds, thinking that such actions will drive out the evil spirits. When the spirits leave the person the Indian women rush at them and pretend to shoot them or stab them with knives. As they do so they are singing and imploring their gods for help. All this is enough to make a healthy person sick. One day I was in a tent where an Indian woman was in labor. She had been suffering many hours, and these medicine men were rattling their gourds and singing. Her husband soon came in and started cutting little images out of stained hide. He would then stand at the door of the tent and throw a piece of hide at her as the occasion arose. He expected this to assist nature in bringing forth the child.

I felt sorry for these poor superstitious beings. Very few of them believe in any god besides a painted stone or stick. Should we expect these creatures to act with reason and judgment as we do?

Think for a minute of all they have borne for years, and you will wonder, as I did, that they saved as many lives as they did. Their religion teaches them to do evil for evil, good for good, and right for right. Many ask me why they killed so many that had befriended them. I asked myself that question many times while I was with them, and here is one answer that I received.

An Indian once went to some white settlers to trade some ducks for some potatoes. The ducks were fresh and good, but the settlers took them and gave the Indian potatoes not fit for a hog to eat. This is how many white settlers befriended the Indians, by giving them what the settlers would never eat themselves. The Indians have been treated this way for years. I know the Indians have killed whites, and I hope every guilty one will be punished. However, I cannot blame the Indians as many people do, for I know they had they had good reasons for taking revenge on people who had been living off their lands and money while the Indians were starving. If these Indians had started an outbreak of violence purely out of wickedness, I would feel different. But this is not what happened; they acted in the only way they knew to get restitution, and we all want that when we have been wronged.

I have very many loyal and good friends among the Indians, and I feel just as much sorrow for them as I would for my white friends. I have listened many times to their stories of suffering and distress until my heart has ached for them. I pray to God that in the future those with authority over the Indians will deal more mercifully with them than they have until now.

Our night passed without an attack by Little Crow and his Indian soldiers. The camp commander had asked us to stay where we were and said that he and his soldiers would come to us. We were getting very impatient now, and our Indian friends said that they might as well leave and not wait any longer. About noon on the third day, we saw the white soldiers coming to our camp. I didn't feel much joy when I saw them, but I was angry, for there were enough soldiers to have come to our rescue before now.

While the white soldiers were advancing, we saw a party of Indians near us. Several half-Indians and some of the Indians went out to meet them and discovered that they were a party of Sissetons. The Sissetons had three prisoners with them, one girl and two boys, whom the Sissetons said they were going to kill. One of our party grabbed the girl and some other Indians in our party grabbed the boys; the Sissetons ran away. I talked with the girl for a while and she said that they had often been so near to the white soldiers that they could hear the soldiers' voices. They crawled on their knees most of the time so the white soldiers wouldn't see them. She had blisters all over her feet, but the Indians had carried the boys part of the way. It seems strange that the Indians should save so many help-less children and murder their parents. The children are so much trouble to the Indians. I have seen Indian women carry white children nine or ten miles on their backs while they let their own children walk. The Indians did this out of their good feelings for the children, for they had no selfish motives in carrying the children this way. The world does the Indians a great injustice when they say they saved people only for selfish reasons.

As the white soldiers came nearer, the Indians grew worried and went into their tents. We were all eager to get to the soldiers, but we were told to stay where we were until the commander came to our camp. The soldiers camped just about a quarter of a mile away, and the commander said he would come over after dinner and talk with the Indians.

About this time some Indian women brought me a dress that belonged to another white woman. How strange God's ways are! I did not think that when I helped her make this dress that I would ever be wearing it, especially under such circumstances. She was dead, and where was I? I was in this camp of Indians and did not know whether or not they would murder me, for I had to travel many miles before I reached civilization.

For the last time, I ate dinner with my Indian friends. They were very sad, and they were afraid of some evil. At about three o'clock the commander and his staff arrived. After talking for a few minutes with the Indians, the commander ordered Indians who had prisoners to bring them out and give them up. Chaska came for me, and before I left his mother tore her shawl and gave me half, for I did not have one.

Trembling with fear, Chaska said, "You are a good woman; you must talk good to your white people, or they will kill me. You know I am a good man and did not shoot Mr. Gleason. You know I saved your life. If I had been a bad man, I would have gone with those bad chiefs." I assured him he didn't have to be afraid, for white soldiers would not hurt him. My promises were all in vain, however, for the whites deceived him right up to his death.

After I was introduced to the commander, he asked me to point out the man who had saved me. Chaska came forward as I called his name, and when I told them how kind Chaska had been, they shook hands with him and made quite a hero of him for a short time. I had to leave this small circle to take care of my baby, and I went to a nearby tent. The white soldiers took the white women with them, and three officers stayed behind to escort me to their camp. When I got to the camp, the soldiers were very excited, and they were all eager to see us. They took me to a large tent that was soon surrounded by soldiers. We nearly suffocated in there. There were twenty-four people in my tent, and we had no bedding. Although they had had many weeks to prepare to rescue us, they had not made any provision for us. My children got very sick, and I wished many times that I were sleeping in an Indian tent. Let me make myself clear. I did not want to live my life among the Indians again; I only wanted the comforts of an Indian tent, for I was much more comfortable with the Indians in every respect than I was during my stay in the soldiers' camp. The Indians treated me with much more respect than the soldiers. We had to cook our own food while exposed to the gaze of several hundred ignorant men. They would surround our fires as soon as we started cooking so that we had no air to breathe. Many times I had to go to an officer and ask for someone to guard us so we could cook without interference. My life with the Indians was much different; the Indian women did all the cooking, unless I wanted to help them.

The nights were now very cold. Although our tent was built so it could have a stove in it, we had none. Sometimes we would make a fire on the ground, but we had to lie down with our faces on the ground because the smoke was so thick.

I had one gingham dress, one cotton skirt, no underwear, and one pair of moccasins. I had no stockings and only half a shawl. I am a large woman, and the Indian women could not find any clothes that would be large enough for me. Before my captivity I had weighed 203 pounds. When I got to Shakopee, eight weeks after my captivity, I weighed 163 pounds. My travels and anxieties had caused me to lose so much.

The first evening I stayed at Camp Release was very pleasant. The soldiers serenaded us and brought us many treats. I believe they thought that we must not have eaten anything for weeks, judging by the amount of treats they brought to us. My children never experienced hunger in the Indian camp, for food was always plentiful. Nearly every day the Indians brought the English doctor's wife some kind of treat. I really thought my children would get sick from eating all the food that the Indians brought them.

The Indian family I was with was not the unkempt, impoverished Indians we used to see begging around our camp. There is a great difference in these two tribes of Indians, and any person visiting the Agency would have been astonished to see such hardworking men and women. These Indians were as clean and neat as our own farmers. I have employed Indian women in my family who were educated by the missionaries. They could read and write in their own language, and make coats, pants, or shirts better than many young white girls who are not being taught these skills.

I always had a towel, soap, and wash dish in my Indian tent. I never knew any member of the family who would neglect to wash and comb before eating a meal. I had my own corner of the tent, and they respected my privacy. I did get very tired of sitting in one place with my baby, for they would not allow me to cross the room to the other side. My little boy, however, enjoyed his life there very much. I used to raise the door to the tent and watch him play happily with the Indian boys. I often asked my son if he wanted to see his father. He told me that he wished his father would come to the Indian camp, for he would have liked to stay there if he could have.

One morning after I had arrived at Camp Release I went back to the Indians' camp for some things I had left there. While I was there I went to a Dakota prayer meeting. Chaska was very frightened. He called me to the door and told me they had arrested two Indians. He said he would know I had lied about him if the soldiers arrested him. He told me that he would lie, too, if he were arrested.

I told him I had had a long talk with one of our officers, and that the officer had said that Chaska should be pardoned because he had been so kind to my children and me. Chaska appeared to be very pleased, and I went back to Camp Release. The commander and his officers held a court of inquiry at which we were all questioned. I was the first one they questioned. I told them all that I have already written in my narrative here. They thought it was strange that I had no complaints to make to them. They did not appear to believe my story. They told me I could leave, but I went to the Indian camp. I sent for Chaska, who looked very pale and frightened. He said the white men were not keeping their promises, and he knew they would kill him. I tried to persuade him to leave, promising to take care of his mother. He said, "No; I am no coward. I am not afraid to die. All I care about is my poor mother; she will be left alone." He said he was sorry that I had persuaded him to stay; his mother was very angry with me for not letting him go. I still held out strong hope to him, insisting that he was going to be spared.

Soon after I left him he was arrested. At first I wasn't too concerned, for I was sure he would be freed. That evening many of the officers were in our tent, and we were all sitting around laughing and talking. We were all acting like little children let out of school early, and we really weren't thinking about the things we said to each other. One of the officers said, "We have seven of the black devils, and before tomorrow night they will be hanged." I asked if they were including the Indian who had protected me. "Yes," he said, "and he will swing with the rest." Without thinking what I was saying, I told the officer that if Chaska were hanged then I would shoot the officer.

I was greatly mystified about the way our camp commander conducted his affairs with the Indians. He took a very long time to march to our Indian camp, wasting many days—or so it seems to me—in his quest to rescue the white prisoners. If those officers had known that their wives and daughters were in danger, I'm sure they would have found ways to travel more than five miles a day. In addition, the commander showed no interest in pursuing Little Crow and his band of murderous Indians. Why did he spend many days trying the Indians who had waited two days to give themselves up willingly to the white soldiers? I can never give the commander any credit for capturing the Indians or for releasing the prisoners. Is it really a capture when the Indians wait two days and nights for their captors to march twenty-five miles? God influenced those Indians to remain with us, and I give great thanks to God and the Indians, but none to the camp commander.

I was very unhappy when I heard Chaska was in prison. I felt as if both the Indians and I had been deceived. All the solemn promises I made to Chaska had been empty. What would he think of me? I could not eat or sleep, for I was so concerned about him. I felt as bad as if my brother were in Chaska's place.

Because they knew how sad I felt, the women tried every way they could to aggravate me by saying, "I know he is a murderer. I know he killed my brother." I said, "If he has done such things, how could you be so friendly with him?" For these same women would often come in and sing, laugh, and play cards with him. One of them used to comb his hair and arrange his ties. After he was arrested, she turned her back on him and said terrible things about him.

They called me in to testify when Chaska was tried. I told them all that I would say would be in Chaska's favor. They thought it was strange that I would speak so favorably of an Indian. I went into court and was put under oath. Chaska was in the room, and I shook hands with him. I told the court honestly how he had helped me and protected me.

He was convicted of being an accomplice in Mr. Gleason's murder, even though there was no evidence against him. I was very angry, for it seemed to me as if they did not even consider my testimony to be worthwhile at all. If they had listened to me and believed what I said, they would have acquitted him. All the evidence they had was his own statement in which he said that he snapped his gun at Mr. Gleason. However, they misrepresented his statement, and made it appear that Chaska had intended to kill Mr. Gleason.

I know he did not intend to kill that man any more than I did. He was present and so was I; that is all. They might as well hang me, for he was as innocent as I am.

After Mr. Gleason was dead and as we rode away from his body, I heard Chaska say to Hapa, "Get out and shoot him again; don't leave him to suffer." Hapa said, "You have not shot today; you go with me, and I will go." They both got out and went to the body, but it was still and motionless. Hapa fired at him, and Chaska raised his gun. I don't believe his gun was loaded at all. His statement was what convicted him, though. When he spoke to me about all of this, Chaska said he was simply doing as he wished someone might do for him. He was afraid Mr. Gleason might have some life left in him, and he wanted to put Mr. Gleason out of his suffering.

After he was convicted I said many things that I probably shouldn't have said, and I might not have said these things during ordinary times. Everyone should know that my mind was in a dreadful state, living as I had for six weeks in continual fear and anxiety. I was incapable of acting rationally. The Indian who saved George Spencer's life was treated as a hero and praised to the skies. I could not help saying that I thought my life and my children's lives were just as valuable as Mr. Spencer's. Why did the Indian who saved us have to be imprisoned while the Indian being celebrated as a great hero had actually murdered many whites?

I soon discovered that the commission was not acting according to justice but according to favor. I was terribly angry with them for such injustice. The angrier I got, the more I talked, and I made matters worse for Chaska and for me. At the camp they soon began to say that I was in love with Chaska and that I was his wife. They said I preferred living with him to living with my husband, and made other accusations just as horrible. I know I am innocent and that I was acting out of right and pure motives. I am sure that if I am condemned here on earth, God will set things right for me, if not here, then in heaven.

I could never love a savage, though I could certainly respect any or all who might befriend me. I would willingly do anything in my power to help those who were so kind to me in my great hour of need. I have strong feelings of gratitude toward many of them. I cannot feel toward the Indians as many people do, for I did not lose any friends, and I was treated kindly by all of them but Hapa. I feel very sorry for any who have suffered at the Indian's hands. I do not know more than two women who were raped by the Indians. I often asked other prisoners, when we met, if they were being well treated. Although we all heard rumors to the contrary, these prisoners all said that the Indians had treated them well.

About two days before I left Camp Release I went to the Indian camp with another white woman. When I saw Chaska's mother she put her arms around me crying, "My boy, my boy! They will kill him! Why don't you save him? He saved your life many times. You have forgotten the Indians now that your white friends have come." Her words greatly affected me, and I told her I was doing everything I could to save him, but that the Indians were telling lies about him. She told me that she had tried to take some bread to him, but that the soldiers would not let her near him. She begged me to go and see him. I had not been to see the prisoners until that day, although the women were going in several times a day to see them. I had always refused, for I knew I would be very sad to see those who had been so kind to me so mistreated by the whites. I felt that the Indians would blame me for not trying to help them now that they were in trouble.

Later this day, I returned to camp and went to the prisoners' tent. When I walked over to Chaska to shake hands, he would not take my hand. I asked him why he was acting so unfriendly. He told me that I must have told lies to the soldiers or he would not be tied up like he was. He then repeated all he had done for my children and me, and chided me for forgetting his kindness so soon. His words moved me to tears, for he spoke of many things he had done such as selling his coat for flour and sleeping without his blanket so my children could be warm. I told him I had lost all my friends by trying to save him, and that he was very wrong to blame me. I am not ashamed to tell you how much I cried then, for I am naturally very sensitive and cannot see someone crying or listen to reproaches without crying myself.

I am convinced I am not to blame for his imprisonment. I told him that I wanted to shake hands and tell him goodbye in friendship. He shook hands with me. I never saw him again, for I left very soon for my home.

There were twenty-one Indians tied together that day I visited Chaska. I was not able to get very close to him, but people have circulated terrible rumors about my visit to him. If anyone doubts my story, they may ask any one of the Indians or other women who were there with me that day. I was unaware of the excitement that existed around the country over the Indians. I knew awful murders had been committed, but I didn't know any of the details or how deeply angry the people were at the Indians. I was so happy over my safe deliverance from death and dishonor because of the Indians' kindness, that I wanted to sing their praises far and near.

Before I left that night, one of the officers told me that Chaska would not be executed but he would be imprisoned for five years. I was content when I heard this, and didn't think about the case any more since the officer gave me his word as a gentleman that this was the truth. He told me not to mention this to anybody since it was a secret. I never told anyone until he was dead.

We left the camp unescorted the next morning. Since we knew there were still Indians in the woods, we were very worried. We had to travel over seventy miles in such a way, and we were all afraid that we would be taken prisoner again or murdered. Once we came to an Indian village that Little Crow had abandoned. Since we were hungry we started to collect some food from the gardens, and we fed our horses some corn while we were there resting. Although we had a few incidents with the Indians along the way to the fort, we finally arrived safely there about five o'clock in the evening. We were very tired but very happy to be within the walls of the fort. I had a refreshing bath, and the clean clothes that one of the fort's women gave me felt so good. I felt great joy as I laid my children down to rest and undressed for sleep. This was the first time in eight weeks that I had changed my clothes to sleep.

The next morning my little boy cried out, "There is my father!" There was my husband whom I had grieved over as dead. He was now alive and walking toward me. I was so happy then, and I felt as if I could have died willingly right there and then. I prayed that the Lord's will, not mine, be done, for I knew my children now had a protector.

I left the fort about noon that day and arrived in Shakopee in a few days. I did not hear any more about Chaska, but felt as if all was well with him. I was in Red Wing when I saw a list of those to be executed. I noticed an Indian named Chaskadon was on the list, but I knew that Chaska was not to be executed for the crime for which this Chaskadon was to be punished.

Sunday after the execution, when the papers were brought in, I noticed my name immediately. I saw then that a mistake had been made. The president had ordered Chaskadon to be hanged, for he had killed a pregnant woman and cut out her child. Instead, they hanged Chaska, who was convicted only of being present when Mr. Gleason was killed.

After about eight weeks in Red Wing, I went to St. Paul. I talked to a former missionary among the Sioux who had been there when Chaska was hanged. He told me that Chaska really was hanged by mistake, as Chaska's name had been on the list of those who were to receive mercy. When the name was called on that morning, he answered to it and walked out. The former missionary didn't think anyone was to blame, and he regretted very much the mistake.

I will never believe that the authorities there forgot what Chaska was condemned for, and I am sure it was done intentionally. I don't dare say who killed him, but there is One who knows every secret, and the time will come when the murderer will meet that murdered man. He will then find the poor Indian's place is far better than his own.

I don't see how such a mistake could have been made. Every prisoner was numbered as he was arrested, and the president would have sent the number as well as the cause of the punishment. I have started to think very unkindly toward my own people because of this event. All kinds of gossip have circulated about Chaska and me, but I don't even listen to it. I know that what I did was right, and that my feelings grew out of my gratitude for what my preserver had done for my children and me. I would have done the same thing for the blackest man that Africa ever produced. I did not love the man, but I loved his kind acts.

I could speak about many things in this narrative, but I would have to mention particular names, and I do not wish to do so. I will say, though, that many people told very different stories about their treatment by the Indians after they went back to the whites than they did before the white soldiers came. One lady who visited me very often said that she always had too much to eat. The Indian women always forced her to eat because they showed kindness and hospitality to people by feeding them well. Now I have listened to her telling the soldiers many times that the Indian women nearly starved her to death. Such lies shocked me, and I reprimanded her severely for telling such lies. She was only one of a class of women who tried to excite the soldiers' sympathy. I tried, on the other hand, to arouse sympathy for the Indians, and the soldiers lost all respect for me. They treated me shamefully. I would rather have my own conscience than that of those who turned against their protectors who had treated them so kindly in that great time of danger.

All the time I was with the Indians the women seemed to envy me. They said that the Indians thought more of me than of any other woman. They did of course think more of me than they did of strangers, for they had known me many years. I could talk with them about things that had happened in Shakopee, and they thought of me as an old friend. No Indian ever came to my house hungry without being fed. If she needed clothes, I gave them to her if I could. They all came to me as frequently as to my husband to get medicine. Their actions have proved the truth of the Bible to me: "Send out your bread upon the waters, for after many days you will get it back" (Ecclesiastes 11:1).

The Indians have always been kind to me, and I continue to take them food and other little things I know will please them. I have been blamed for this, but I cannot help it. In God's own time my conduct will be understood and I will be justified, for with God all things are plain. And now I say goodbye to this subject forever.

CHRISTIAN CLASSICS FROM PARACLETE PRESS

Living Love: A Modern Edition of Treatise on the Love of God
Francis de Sales

Ascent of Mount Carmel
John of the Cross

The Confessions of St. Augustine

The Imitation of Christ
Thomas à Kempis

The Practice of the Presence of God
Brother Lawrence

Eternal Wisdom from the Desert Writings of the Desert Fathers

The Pilgrim's Progress
John Bunyan

The Joy of Full Surrender
Jean-Pierre de Caussade

The Way of Perfection
Theresa of Avila

Little Talks with God
Catherine of Siena

Meditations on the Heart of God
François Fénelon

Talking with God
François Fénelon

The Royal Way of the Cross
François Fénelon

Religious Poetry and Prose
John Donne

The Temple
The Poetry of George Herbert

Holy Living
Jeremy Taylor

Life Secrets
Henry Foster

Talks on the Song of Songs
Bernard of Clairvaux

Religion of the Heart
Hannah Moore

Lead, Kindly Light
John Henry Newman